For Posterity

A Letter to My Children

by

Russell H. Volkema

to
Jay and Marie
from
Russell Volkema

DORRANCE PUBLISHING CO., INC.
PITTSBURGH, PENNSYLVANIA 15222

ISBN #0-8059-4049-9
Printed in the United States of America

First Printing

For information or to order additional books, please write:
Dorrance Publishing Co., Inc.
643 Smithfield Street
Pittsburgh, Pennsylvania 15222
U.S.A.

Dedication

This book is dedicated to my wife and to my deceased mother and brother "B", each of whom have been an inspiration to me and have had a definite impact upon my life.

Contents

Chapter I.

Salutation

Dear Colette, Daniel, Michael, & Kimberly:

Lately, for some mystical reason, I am curious about my roots. Maybe it's because I have a little more time to concentrate on such matters now that I have reduced my responsibilities within my law office, or maybe it's because I see myself as a vital link in a human chain that is responsible for your existence, or perhaps it's just natural when a person passes the half-century mark that there emerges an innate desire to take an in-depth look at his or her heritage. Details about the nature and background of one's parents are generally of special interest. With my natural inclination to repeat old stories, and with the urging and encouragement of your mother for me to set forth some personal data for the sake of posterity, I have decided to couch an overview of my pre-marriage life for each of you to review when you reach an inquiring age.

My father, Andrew Volkema, whom I knew as "Pa," was born Aan Symens Fokkema on August 7, 1890. (The "s" in Symens means "child of." Pa was therefore the son of Symen) His birthplace was a farm near the quaint little village of Rinsumageest (pronounced Rhine-sue-ma-gayest) which was, and is, near the North Sea in Friesland, The Netherlands. (Friesland is the Dutch spelling. Fryslan is the Friese spelling). He was the ninth of thirteen children.

Pa's parents were Symen Fokkes Fokkema (American name Simon Frank Volkema) (1852 - 1927) and Eelkje Dirks (1854 - 1937). His mother's maiden name was Eelkje Dirks Algra.

It is interesting to note from the certificate which my grandparents used for emigration purposes that every child's middle name, whether a boy or a girl, was the father's first name, with an "s" attached. It was the custom in the Netherlands at that time to give each child of a family the father's first name as a middle name. This was probably for the purpose of tracing the history of each person. Accordingly, and obviously, every Fokkema with a middle name of Symens was a descendant of Symen. Pa's parents broke with this tradition when they arrived in America, where they gave their last child, Dorothy, the middle name of Hendrike. Also in the Netherlands every name given to a child had to be approved by the government.

Pa's grandfather (Pake in Friese) was Fokke Jacobs Fokkema (1811 - 1888). His great-grandfather was Jacob Fokkes Fokkema (1784 - 1828). His great-great-grandfather was Fokke Jacobs (dates unknown).

You undoubtedly have observed that the father of Jacob Fokkes Fokkema, Fokke Jacobs, only had two names. The practice of having two names was accepted during the time of Fokke Jacobs. A person generally had a first identifying name and a second name that would reveal who his or her father was. However, when the Netherlands came under French control during the Napoleonic era, around 1811, the subjects were required to have a surname. In keeping with this mandate, the son of Fokke Jacobs, Jacob Fokkes Fokkema,

De Gereformeerde kerk, gebouwd 1888.
The Reformed (secessionist) Church which was built in 1888 in Rinsumageest.
My father, Aan Fokkema, was baptized in this church in September, 1890.

evidently took his second name, Fokkes, and added the suffix "ma," and used it for a last name. The old genitive suffix "ma" meant either "son of" or "belonging to the family of." The name Fokkema thereupon became the family name. Many other subjects of that time in Friesland must have done likewise inasmuch as many Frieslanders have last names that end in "ma."

All of Pa's brothers and sisters were born in the Netherlands, except Dorothy, as previously stated, who was born in Grand Rapids, Michigan, in 1895. Pa's father was tall and sturdy in appearance. Pa's mother was small, about 5'3" in height, and rather slim. All of Pa's brothers and sisters were about 5'4" - 5'9" and slightly built, except his brother George, who had a relatively large bone structure and was about 5'10".

The Fokkema family was attracted to the Grand Rapids area because other families from the Netherlands who were known to them had emigrated from the Netherlands to this part of America.

I cannot remember much of what was told to me over the years about the transatlantic voyage of this large family from the Netherlands to the United States. I do recall hearing that Pa was about four years old when he landed in this country. The date of the emigration records supports this fact, as does the fact that two children younger than Pa were also born in the Netherlands.

It was, no doubt, a trying ordeal for my grandparents and their large family to cross the Atlantic in what must have been an antiquated ship with substandard accommodations. Organization of such a large group, which included several small children, in order to render adequate care relating to the necessities of life, had to be an almost impossible task.

I don't remember ever seeing my grandfather. I did see and visit Pa's mother during her latter years. She was a small woman, with a wrinkled face. Whenever we would stop in to visit her, she would have a pot of coffee on the stove ready to serve. Generally when Pa and I would stop at her tiny house, which was in the back yard of the home of one of her other sons, there would be one or more of Pa's bothers or sisters, or some nephew or niece, already there, visiting with Grandma. She enjoyed socializing with her kinfolk.

It was not especially interesting for me to sit and wait at Grandma's little house while Pa would converse in Friese and slowly drink his coffee. Sometimes the verbal exchange among those visiting would be a mixture of Dutch, Friese, and English. I could generally get the gist of the conversation when they would use this interplay of languages. From their gibberish chatter I learned about the problems of the day and the hardships that the family had endured.

I know very little about the family tree of my father's mother (Beppe in Friese). I do know that her maiden name was Eelkje Dirks Algra and that she was the daughter of Dirk Aans Algra and Niienke Boonstra. I believe they were also from Rinsumageest.

I have been told that Pa's parents had a difficult time surviving after they arrived in Michigan. They soon expended the money that they had taken with them from the "old country," and there was no reserve for long term needs. Because of this, their children were forced to shift for themselves at an early age and grew up with minimal supervision. Pa was only educated through the third grade at a local school. Not being academically inclined, he never made much advancement in this area of his life. He acquired a very limited ability to read. He never developed an ability to write. To my knowledge, Pa never wrote a letter during his entire lifetime. This lack of education and lack of development had an adverse impact upon his life and upon the life of his family.

As a boy, Pa lived on Century Avenue in Grand Rapids, Michigan. It was a street that ran in a northerly and southerly direction along the railroad tracks. A few blocks to the west of the Fokkema home lived a family by the name of Reminga. The Reminga family had one daughter and three sons. The daughter became my mother. Her parents' names were Neal and Sarah Reminga (Sarah's maiden name was Sarah Doelder). My mother's maiden name was Hazel Reminga. I only knew her as "Ma." Her brothers' names were Harry, Neal, and Daniel. Ma was the oldest child.

I have no information regarding the Reminga or Doelder family tree. I do, however, know that Ma's father was born in the Netherlands and that her mother was born in the United States. Her parents could understand some Dutch, but they never spoke it in their home. Consequently, Ma never learned the Dutch language. She therefore was unable to converse with Pa in Dutch. Because of this, neither I nor my brothers and sisters ever learned to speak or understand the Dutch or Frisian language.

I never knew my grandfather Reminga, but I heard enough about him to learn some things regarding his character and abilities. He was an intelligent and well-informed person and a master craftsman in the furniture business. He was highly skilled in his specialty, which was in the finishing of furniture. But he had a serious problem — he was an alcoholic. As a result of this, the family was constantly plagued with money problems. Grandma Reminga took in washing and boarders to keep the family alive.

Ma was the only daughter in the Reminga family. The possibilities of evolving out of such an environment in that day and age were very bleak. She got some odd jobs doing housework. At the age of sixteen she got a job in the Alabastrine Company sacking fertilizer. It was hard and dusty work.

Uncle Dan, Ma's brother, (who at the time of this writing of this letter is still living) told me about my mother when she was working at the Alabastrine Company. He said she was the type of person who assumed that everyone was honest. While working at her job she began to question the procedure of putting the same ingredients from the same barrel into three different-colored sacks. Each sack was differently priced. One day she asked her boss, "How come we put the same stuff in these different-priced bags?" The boss, in response, put his finger to his mouth and said, "s-h-h-h." She simply could not understand why a company would want to cheat people. But she was poor and just new on the job; so she asked no more questions.

My uncle also told me that Ma, as a girl, was an intelligent, alert, and friendly person. She was an excellent student who had many girlfriends. Among her friends were the younger sisters of Pa. She went to some of the lower grades in school with them, and together they also attended a young people's church group in the local area. Through this medium she met Pa at a young age. She was four years younger than her boyfriend "Andy." Their relationship overheated at an early age in an uncontrolled environment. The result was a marriage of necessity. Her youth was cut short. She married "Andy" at the age of seventeen, and they began their married life by living and working in the city. Her first child, a son named Francis, was born about seven months after their marriage. Following the birth of Francis, there were Dorothy, Ethel, Russell (5/23/20), and Andrew, Jr.

All the children were born in Grand Rapids except me. I was born on a farm about two miles southeast of Moline, Michigan. Pa's brother Charles, who lived a few miles to the northwest of this farm, had encouraged Pa to purchase the farm and to commute back and forth to work at the factory in Grand Rapids on what was called the Interurban Train. The farm and farm house are still intact, with some modification.

I have been told that things got pretty rough on the Moline farm. My brother Francis, who was nicknamed "Chic," told me several times how he had to walk the distance of a few miles to the town of Moline to get ten cents worth of bologna. There was generally only enough money in the house to buy that amount of meat at one time.

In later life Chic used to kid my sister Dorothy about not wanting to walk home with the rest of the kids on a certain day from the one-room schoolhouse which they both attended while we lived on this farm. The little grade school was about a mile away. Dorothy evidently took off through the fields by herself one day after school because she had dirtied her pants. She wanted no one to know about it. Chic never let her forget it. Dorothy later became a teacher in a nearby and similar one-room schoolhouse, earning $35 per month.

My birth on the farm was a frightening event for everyone involved. Ma turned blue during delivery and nearly died. A neighbor lady by the name of Mrs. Spykerman had been called in to help as a midwife. No doctor was available. This fourth unplanned addition to the family and the disenchantment of the farm-factory venture motivated Ma and Pa to move back to the city.

Chapter II.

Boyhood Days In The City

Pondering the move from the city to the Caledonia farm.

After returning to the city, Pa continued to work at the factory known as Leonards. In addition to this employment, and as a supplemental means of making a living, he began to huckster fruits and vegetables, first with a horse and wagon and later with a Model "T" truck which had a specially built rack to display the produce. Finances became somewhat stabilized. The debt on the family home routinely diminished. Security was just around the corner. Pa even had time to give free haircuts to the nearby children of a needy family. He was not a barber, but he gave pretty good cuts; at least the mother of the poor kids appreciated them.

One of the regular recipients of these free cuts refused to return for barber services. The reason, as I remember it, was this: every Halloween some pranksters would creep up behind our outdoor privy during the middle of the night and tip it over. Finally, Pa, with the help of a neighbor, moved the outhouse a few feet forward, the width of the foundation on which it normally sat. He then placed some straw and leaves over the exposed refuse. During the night the Halloween prowlers made their regular rounds. As they ran up to tip our privy over, they fell into three feet of dung. This nasty trick caught one of the free-hair-cut recipients. He was so infuriated by the whole ordeal that he thereafter refused Pa's gratuitous services.

In the midst of what appeared to be a general normalization of family life, my brother Andrew, Jr., the last child, was born on February 16, 1922. To Ma and Pa it was a shock that would last for more than fourteen years. It took a short while for them to become cognizant of the realities involved. My brother Chic best described the first submission by my mother to the realization that Andrew, Jr., would be permanently deformed. He said he was at the neighbor's house across the street (at the corner of Evergreen Avenue and Burton Street) from where the bus stop was located. He saw Ma get off the bus with my little brother, Andrew, Jr., ("B" as he was later nicknamed) in her arms. She was returning from the doctor's office, where she evidently had been informed about the reality of his condition. As soon as she disembarked from the bus and got her footing, she ran toward our house, which was about a half block away, crying, with B in her arms. The catastrophic and permanent deformity that was little B's destiny was without a doubt a blow to the very underpinning of the family structure. B, from that point on, was the center of the family's attention and concern, and rightly so.

My uncle Dan, Ma's youngest brother, recently described to me the appearance of B when he first saw him. He said he hardly looked human. His legs were about as skinny as a person's little finger. He had no strength in his neck or in any of his limbs. Uncle Dan expressed to me what his thoughts were about the whole ordeal at the time B was born. He said he was furious at the medical doctors for having allowed such a child to live. Uncle Dan has always been, and still is, an advocate of euthanasia in such cases. Ma knew of her brother's thoughts and opinions on the matter. She did not appreciate them.

Not too long after the birth of B, Pa and Ma brought all five of their children before the baptismal font at the nearby Eighth Reformed Church, where we were all baptized.

B grew to a height of about three and one-half feet. He was restricted during his entire life with a weakly, deformed, and frail body. He never went to school. He never learned to read. However, he was alert and quite intelligent. Only his family could understand his speech. He lived fourteen years and sixteen days. He was the first of the family to die. His death came on July 2, 1936.

It was during my life on Evergreen Avenue in Grand Rapids (Galewood), Michigan that I began to accumulate memories through experiences and observations. I remember my mother being a friend of the wife of the minister of the Eighth Reformed Church, Mrs. Menning. Reverend and Mrs. Menning had a son, Bob. He was my age, about five.

Bob and I used to play together around the church. One day Ma came looking for me because I had been gone for an extended period of time. She and Mrs. Menning started to call for us from the back steps of the parsonage, which was next to the church. They probably were worried about our safety because of a nearby ravine. Bob and I entered into a full-blown conspiracy to make them deeply concerned about our absence. We deliberately failed to respond to their call, even though we were right next to the house in the garage. We kept exceedingly quiet. We were definitely deceptive. Finally, when our mothers were seemingly at their wits' end, we dashed out of the garage with great laughter and satisfaction in having caused them a great deal of distress.

On another occasion I had been at the church grounds playing, when I suddenly decided to run across Burton Street in order to return home. Without looking, I darted into the street, only to be run over by a Model "T" Ford. The wheels were so high on the old Model "T" that the car somehow passed over me without inflicting too many bruises. I was frightened by the ordeal and immediately ran home, which was about a half a block away, and hid in our garage. The driver came looking for me. He, along with my mother, found me in the garage nursing my wounds.

I also remember an encounter with a train when I was visiting my cousins, Harold and Simon Folkema. (Their father, Frank, changed his last name from Fokkema to Folkema, whereas my father and his brothers changed their last name to Volkema). Harold and Simon lived on Clyde Park Avenue, only a few blocks to the east of our home. A few blocks back of their home was a train track. Occasionally we would wander over to the track area hoping to have some fun. One day a slow-moving train was crossing Burton Street. Even though I was only about five years old, I hopped on the ladder on the side of a boxcar. When I did this, about three drivers of cars, who were waiting for the train to pass, blew their horns. This rebuff to my venture scared me, so I jumped off. It was a good thing that I did, as the train kept on going.

My closest scrape with death while living on Evergreen Street was when I accompanied Pa on his huckster route with his new Model "T" truck. He always stopped in at his sister Nellie's home for coffee. When I heard him returning to the truck I decided to start the truck for him. I put both the spark and gas lever in a down position. This, unbeknownst to me, was not in accordance with the normal starting procedure. The spark should be down only slightly in order to avoid a "kicking" of the crank. With the spark and gas way down I pulled the crank. It kicked me in the head. It split my head wide open and indented my skull. The next thing I knew I was in the hospital with a completely bandaged head. I enjoyed the attention that I received at the hospital.

My early school days were spent in the Godfrey Avenue grade school. I don't remember much about the old brick school, but I do remember one occasion. It was the policy in those days to hold up one finger if you wanted to ask permission to leave the room to urinate and two fingers for a bowel movement. My teacher evidently got tired of the students leaving the room so frequently; so the teacher made a rule for the rest of the day — no more leaving the room. I was in a dilemma. I was a bed wetter and a person who had to urinate frequently. The prohibition order made me all the more anxious. I soon raised my finger, whereupon the teacher took me out of the room and beat me unmercifully. I was black and blue over several parts of my body. I could walk home but only with a great amount of pain. Ma and Pa talked about the matter but, to my knowledge, they did nothing about it. For a considerable time thereafter I was afraid to attend class.

My part in a church Christmas program was probably one of the most embarrassing encounters of my life during that young age. All the five-year-olds were to sing a song. I rose from my seat with the rest of the class and marched from the pew section in the sanctuary to the elevated pulpit area where we were to show off our talents. I climbed the six or seven steps to the pulpit area without difficulty. But once I got there and saw the crowd I encountered stage fright. I broke ranks and zeroed in on a nearby corner on the pulpit and put my back to the audience. The rest of the "dummies" sang real well. After having sung the song, all the kids started marching back down to the pews. When I realized they were leaving the pulpit area, I zipped into line in order to get out of a terrifying situation. When I marched back up the aisle toward my seat, everyone was looking and laughing at me. The eyes of the people in the audience were as big as saucers, and their broad smiles were insulting. It was some time before I ever regained enough nerve to face an audience.

In 1926 Ma and Pa bought a farm about twenty miles away. It was good to leave some of the bad memories that were trailing me, but to leave my friend Bob, my cousins, and other neighborhood friends was not a pleasant experience. (Many years later when I was serving as a pilot in the U.S. Navy Air Corps during World War II, I was informed that my friend Bob had become an Army pilot and that he had been shot down and was made a prisoner of war in Germany. He and several other prisoners somehow tunneled a passage way out of the prison camp. A movie was made of this. I believe it was called "The Stalag 17").

Chapter III.

Life On The Caledonia Farm

The Caledonia farm.

The actual moving to Pa and Ma's new sixty-acre farm followed the legal transfer of Pa and Ma's house, which was paid for, to the owner of the farm, plus assuming the seller's obligations on an existing first mortgage. The farm was near Caledonia, Michigan. Once the paper work was completed, Ma and Pa loaded their household furnishings on a small moving van. The movers took their belongings to the farm and then loaded the farmer's furnishings on the van and hauled them to the house on Evergreen Avenue. After the moving van left Evergreen Avenue for the farm, Pa, Ma, and the older kids loaded everything possible on top of Pa's 1920 Model "T" Ford Tudor Sedan.

We took off looking like the Grapes of Wrath, but everyone was laughing. We all had an uncontrollable perverse inclination to laugh at ourselves, sometimes even in tragedy. When we got to Cutlerville, and in front of what we called the church's insane asylum, a tire blew. There we all sat half laughing and half crying. (The asylum was a psychopathic hospital. When we would pass this hospital after we moved to the farm, Ma would generally say, "There is one place I never want to go." She later died there at age 57. She suffered extensively from what was then diagnosed as arteriosclerosis. We now believe it was Alzheimer disease.)

When we finally arrived at the farm, there was a lot of excitement. The house was very different. It had no furnace. It was heated with a potbellied stove. There was no heat upstairs, except from a hole in the living room ceiling above the stove, which only serviced the one bedroom. The toilet was in the woodshed. There was no electricity. Kerosene lamps were used both in the house and in the barn. The kitchen had a hand water pump. The tiny milk house, which was only about thirty feet from the back door of the house, had a tiny windmill. The cook stove was an old coal and wood burner. There was, of course, no bath tub.

While we were getting settled in the house, we heard a tractor come up the driveway. Without stopping at the house, a one-armed man swung his tractor and plow into the field next to the driveway. It was our neighbor, Joe Wenger. (His father was a veterinarian who owned the adjoining farm.) Joe plowed the whole field and then stopped at the house to say hello. He knew Pa was behind schedule for getting his crops in. He also knew that Pa was not a farmer and that he only had horses to work with. Joe and the rest of the Wenger family became, and remained, great neighbors.

Parenthetically, I might say that the children of the people who sold my parents the farm also became good friends of my older brother and sisters. My brother Chic became a very close friend of one of the sons of the former owners of the farm. His name was "Chuck." About twenty years later Chuck's wife died. He became involved with Chic's wife when Chic was confined to a sanitarium with tuberculosis. The result was a divorce between Chic and his wife. Chuck thereafter married Chic's ex-wife. It was a bitter encounter for everyone involved. Chic was awarded custody of their five children.

Notwithstanding this upbeat start on the farm that was given to us by our neighbors, the economic situation began to deteriorate, both nationally and personally.

Hard work became a way of life for every member of the family. My sisters, who were city girls, undertook the laborious tasks of milking cows, feeding chickens and livestock, and helping in the fields. To encourage me to work, I was constantly reminded of Jake, a neighbor boy a couple of farms away, who was only six years of age and worked like a man in the fields all day. I was seven, so I too should be giving some thought to working like a man. My responsibilities increased as I grew older. My work started with the feeding of the chickens, bringing the cows up to the barn from the pasture, and picking pickles.

Harvesting the annual pickle crop was a miserable backbreaking event. I hated the job with a passion. As I grew older I would escape the duty whenever possible. But there were some benefits that were associated with this most difficult task.

During pickle-picking time Ma would periodically bring us some freshly made lemonade and set it in the shade under the large oak tree that was in our front yard near the road. The arrival of the refreshments meant a temporary reprieve from the hot sun and dusty field. I have never had a drink that tasted any better than Ma's lemonade which we drank under the old oak tree during those hot summer days.

The most cherished benefit that was associated with pickle-picking time was the opportunity to win a five-pound box of chocolates. The pickle factory, which was a long narrow building with huge open vats on the inside, had a bonus practice whereby farmers would be given a five-pound box of chocolates for every so many thousand pounds of pickles. The purpose of the program was to encourage farmers to increase their yield. We all loved those chocolates.

One year we suffered a real disappointment. Our pickle crop was slim but we thought the harvest was sufficient to warrant the bonus. When the last load was placed on the wagon, I decided to go along with Pa to make the delivery, and, of course, to help carry home the prize. When we arrived at the processing plant in Dutton, there were several wagons ahead of us. I waited on the wagon while Pa went to the store and conversed with other farmers. As the line moved forward I would drive the horses and wagon ahead in order to keep our place in the waiting line. Within a couple of hours it was our turn to unload. I anxiously waited for our weigh-slip. We were short only a few hundred pounds. Pa tried to get the factory owner to bend the rule and give us the chocolates, but he would not alter his incentive program. He refused to give Pa the chocolates.

Everyone at the house was waiting for us to return, with the earnest hope that we would be carrying the goodies. As Pa drove the horses and wagon off the narrow gravel road on to the long sandy driveway that led past the east side of our house and which led to the area of the barn, Ma, little B, and one of my sisters were on the small front porch waiting to find out whether we had earned the box of candy. Their disappointment was self evident when Pa gave the thumbs down signal. They were not only disappointed; they were also disgusted with the wealthy factory owner, who lived on a nearby show farm, for not bending the rule when we were so close to the required poundage. B was the most disheartened. His whole life centered around the success and failure of the family.

When our family became residents of Caledonia Township, I was registered by my parents in a one-room school that was located one mile east and one mile south from our farm. It was located on the northeast corner of an intersection in the country, now known as Kraft Road and 84th Street. The intersection was known as Holy Corners. In addition to our school there was a church on the southwest corner, a graveyard on the northwest corner, and a farmhouse on the southeast corner. That's all that was there.

The name of my school was the Holy Corners School. (I assume the crossroads area got its name because of the church and graveyard). I would walk the entire two miles to this school with the younger brothers of our one-armed neighbor.

On a very cold day as we were walking to school a Greyhound bus stopped for us just as we turned on to the southerly mile. The driver opened the door and invited us in. My neighbor friends were timid kids so I took the initiative and hollered to the driver "We ain't got no money." The driver said he wouldn't make any charge for this ride. This was a good deal. We boarded the bus and sat there like three little kings, glancing back and forth at each other with grins of accomplishment, until we disembarked right next to the school. This gave us an exciting story to tell the teacher, classmates, and, of course, our families.

During the spring of the year I would sometimes cut across the fields and through a maple tree forest. In the center of the forest there was a sugar shack operated by a nearby farmer. "Art" was his name. He used to let me stir the sap. When it became syrup he would give me a taste. When it turned to sugar he would give me some to take home. When the local father-son banquet was held at the Holy Corners Lutheran Church, across from the school, "Art" took me as a son. Pa never went to that sort of thing.

The little one-room school at Holy Corners had a man teacher the first year I attended. He was succeeded by a woman teacher. Both of them were wonderful. The kids at school were also very friendly. However, they acted peculiarly toward a retarded boy who lived about a quarter of a mile north of the school, right along the route I took, whether I walked along the road or across the fields. His name was "Don." He was an adopted boy. The students would thrown things at him and "goose" him in the behind in order to get him to retort with a particular plea to stop. I never joined the kids in this cruel type of humor, but would instead yell at them to quit it. My protective attitude toward handicapped children probably developed because of B's condition. In any event, when I would stand up for Don it would occasionally bring me at odds with some of my peers.

Don looked upon me as a true friend. He felt there was a certain amount of security for him if he waited for me to walk with him to school. When I would leave the school for home, he would be right at my side. If anyone would throw snowballs or other objects at him, I would take up his defense. Unfortunately for Don, I was transferred to French Street School when I passed into the 7th grade. French Street School was only one and one-half miles from our farm, and it was to the west of our farm. I could occasionally get a ride to this school. The neighbor to the west of us, who was the Supervisor of Gaines Township, may have helped my parents get the transfer.

During this period of transition and adjustment from Holy Corners School to French Street School, I began to sense that I was being observed by others as an unruly child. It was generally known among my friends that I would obstinately refuse to move or act in response to parental instruction, would answer them disrespectfully, and would frequently take off for short periods of time to an area where I could not be found. Such conduct on my part was a cross that Ma and Pa should not have had to bear, especially during a time when they were beginning to realize that their life savings were in jeopardy due to a downturn in the national economy.

I was not only a rebellious and insubordinate child, I remained a perpetual bed wetter and a child who suffered repeatedly from chest colds and soreness of the throat.

The bed-wetting problem was never solved during the years we lived on the farm. Because of the problem, I was given a straw tick as my mattress to sleep on. My straw tick was a heavy cloth cover, the size of a mattress, into which straw was placed. About every three or four days someone would help me carry my mattress to the barnyard, where we would empty it. I would then pack the cloth encasement cover the unblemished straw and jump on it until it was reasonably flat. With some help I would get my mattress back into my bedroom. Ma would then cover it with clean sheets which she had washed on her scrub board (her only means of washing her clothes and bedding) and which she dried by hanging them on her outdoor clothes line.

For the chest colds and soreness of the throat, Ma would prepare a mustard plaster. This consisted of a pungent paste prepared from mustard seed, which was placed on a thick cloth. After the paste began to jell, Ma would tie it on my chest. Medicinally it was supposed to heat the chest, penetrate the infected area, and destroy the virus. Sometimes she would apply lard and turpentine on an old piece of flannel and use it in lieu of a mustard plaster. For the soreness of the throat Ma would give me some medicine. To keep me healthy I was given cod-liver oil.

In the midst of all of this gloom there were some exciting memorable times.

My little brother B and I used to play together, notwithstanding his disabilities. When I was about seven years of age, I got a long board, about six feet in length, and attached some discarded tricycle wheels to the bottom of it and made a cart. Almost every day I would put B on the old board-cart and give him a ride around the back yard. After a few of these trips we would play in the sand. Even though I grew much faster than B did as the years went by, B's stunted growth did not diminish our relationship.

B was retarded in many ways. But as I previously stated, he was not dumb. He had a special sound or name for each of his brothers and sisters. Chic was called "Oannh," Dorothy was "Dor," Ethel was "Ato," I was "Caa;" he could say car (caa); so I told him to call me car. He could not say his own name, Andrew; so he was encouraged to pick a name he could pronounce. He could say the letter "B" very easily; so we all decided to call him B. By this means he could give his name to others who would ask him his name.

B had a very exceptional friend while we were on the farm. Our neighbor the township supervisor, and his wife adopted a baby boy. His name was Bobby. The two of them used to play together until Bobby quickly outgrew B. Every little friend B got to know would soon outgrow him. His lasting friends were adults. His favorite uncle was Pa's brother Charles. Uncle Charlie had no children. Whenever he would come to our home he would bring B a little gift.

My personal experience on the farm during the ages of six through fourteen were somewhat unusual. They reveal something about myself and about my upbringing.

When I was approximately eight years of age, I decided it was time for me to leave the family compound. If only I could get a job with someone. I bridled up the old nag and took to the road, determined to find some work. I finally found a farmer who showed some interest in me. He said he had a lot of chickens and two very special roosters. He probably could use me, he said, to lead these two roosters to water each morning just before crowing time. It was years later before I realized that the job offer was adult humor.

Fishing was something I enjoyed as a small boy. When I could break away from field work, with permission or otherwise, I would either hike or ride my old bicycle down to the Thornapple River Dam which was about five miles from our farm. Most of the time I would walk. My rickety old bike had one tire that was filled with oats and couldn't travel very fast with such a tire. Every time I would go to the dam I would catch several little sun fish. Most of my fishing days were not with permission; so I would give my fish to one of my fishing friends to avoid arriving home with evidence of my misbehavior.

A real fisherman is, however, not without pride. On my return home from a permissive day of fishing, I found a large fish, a carp, lying on the shore of the river. Some fisherman before me had evidently caught it and threw it away. Delighted with the find, I threw it over my shoulder and walked along the five miles of roadway toward home. When cars would pass me, the occupants would turn around and look with amazement. This made me exceptionally proud. They thought I was responsible for the huge catch, and I knew what they were thinking. I was disappointed when I arrived home and was instructed to throw the fish away. It was not edible.

Another means of recreation was catching pigeons. I would go to a neighbor's farm where there were a couple of bashful children who were slightly younger than myself. Following a slight strategy meeting, I would climb up one end of the inside of this barn to the very peak. After I would get a good footing, one of my friends would climb up the other end where the pigeons were perched. As he would approach, the pigeons would attempt an escape by flying toward a hole at the opposite end of the barn where I was located. As soon as they would get to my corner, I would grab them and put them in a sack. I would take these captured pigeons home and add them to the number that I would catch in our barn. Pa would then put the pigeons in large open-air crates and peddle (sell) them to immigrants who lived in the inner city. To them, pigeon meat was a delicacy.

Shooting sparrows was also a profitable venture. There was as a bounty on sparrows — two cents a head. I would shoot them with my BB gun, sever their heads, and put them in a bag. When I got a bag full I would cash them in. The bounty was a government-sponsored program for the purpose of controlling the sparrow population. The sparrows were consuming the crops.

Pickle-picking days for me were a time of imprisonment. Everybody had to be in the field. On several occasions I would rebel. Trumping up an excuse to go to the house or barn, I would escape the work area and hook up the old "nag" (horse with heaves) to the buggy and trot off to the nearby town of Dutton, with full knowledge that I would be seriously punished upon return.

During one of my reckless adventures I drove the horse and buggy to Dutton, gathered up a group of friends, and drove a mile southward toward a nearby park where we intended to swim and play. Across the narrow country road from the park lived Charlie, an old spooky-looking bachelor. We boldly circled up into Charlie's circle driveway and shouted, "Hey Charlie!" Charlie opened the door of his house with the speed of lightning and yelled at us to get out of his yard. A quick slap on the back end of the old nag gave us a sudden jerk and a swift exit. When we reached the end of the driveway, we were traveling too fast to make the turn onto the road. An attempted turn caused both our buggy and horse to roll over into the ditch, leaving the buggy and the nag upside down. Fortunately, all of the kids escaped injury; tragedy was again somehow miraculously averted.

On my arrival home, Ma, without knowing anything about this accident, was ready with the stove poker. Whenever I would violate the rules, and if she could catch me, I would get some hard whacks across my behind. I was always cognizant during my escapades that I was exchanging some pleasure for some poker marks.

Smoking was my next venture. Having heard about several of the kids smoking corn silk, I thought I would give it a try. I took some paper and matches and went deep into the corn field, where I got some brown silk, rolled it up like a cigarette, and lit it. I puffed away until the cigarette was about half gone. (Unbeknownst to me, Ma saw the smoke rising about the corn.) After having succeeded in this new experience I headed for the house. As I got near the house, I became nauseated and began to vomit. Ma asked what the trouble was. I of course had no idea what was making me so sick. Ma, with tongue in cheek, said sometimes smoking corn silk would cause such an illness. I wasn't about to admit I had committed that kind of crime.

Sometimes unforeseen consequences would ensue from what was meant to be merely a risky undertaking. In one instance, Pa, in an effort to make a few dollars, would buy wild horses from the west and attempt to train them, "break them," as it was called in those days. He would put a bridle on the horse and a rope around one of the horse's front legs. He would then let the horse out into an open field, holding the reins in one hand and rope in the other hand. If the horse would attempt to run, Pa would holler, "Halt!" At this point he would pull on both the reins and the rope. If the horse wouldn't stop, the horse would trip and fall.

One sunny afternoon in late June, when the corn was a few inches tall in the field next to the barn, I decided to get on the ridge of the silo foundation which was in the barnyard, to see whether or not I could hop on to the back of one of these horses. For my age, about ten, I was an expert horse rider. I had no problems riding without a saddle. When one of the partially trained horses that was in the barnyard neared the foundation of the silo, I jumped onto his back. It was the rodeo of the century. I was thrown to the ground, and all the horses that were in the barnyard leaped the rail fence and ran amuck in the corn field.

Pa's corn field was his pride and joy when it began to grow. Every farmer took pride in squaring off his corn field by means of dragging a pull-marker which was made of wood staves that were placed in a vertical position three feet apart. First he would drag the marker one way across the field and then at a ninety-degree cross angle. A marking job well done would allow a viewer to look straight down the row from different directions. This alignment procedure was done for the purpose of allowing cross-cultivation. Once the field was squared off, Pa and each of us kids would take a stand-up hand planter and place a few kernels of corn in the ground at each intersecting mark. Pa always seemed please when the corn began to grow and the rows seemed to be straight.

I tried to herd the horses back into the barnyard but they would reel around just as they got near the open gate over which they had previously jumped, and would gallop back across the field. It seemed at the time that the horses' steps, whether running or walking, were exactly three feet apart, right on the squares of the growing corn. I was afraid of what Pa would do. Pa was as a non-responsive man who seemed to pay little attention to his family, but when he would get mad at someone he would lose all control of himself.

While I was trying to get the horses back into the barnyard, Pa arrived on the scene. I could see the uncontrollable redness in his face. He immediately joined the effort to get the horses back in the yard. We were doing well, until the horses got near the barnyard gate. When they approached the gate area, they repeated their formerly employed escape procedure and galloped back out into the field, whereupon Pa took out after me. Luckily the horses quickly positioned themselves for another chance to round them up. This time we were successful. I hustled away immediately after Pa put up the rail, in order to keep a safe distance away from him. I went to the back pasture and brought up the cows for milking. On this afternoon I did not mind getting the cows. I always rode on an old black cow when driving the cattle from the field to the barn. It was much easier than walking.

Once the cows were in the barn, I attempted to redeem myself by quickly getting the pails and cans for milking. Pa started first. He placed his milking stool next to a cow while still fuming from the thought of all that corn being ruined. In order to work my way back into some sort of rapport with Pa, I hurried back to the milk house for the rest of the milking pails. When I returned to the barn at top speed I slipped on the floor, causing severe pain between my legs. It was as a dastardly fall. Pa probably thought that medical attention would be needed. He looked, saw me on the floor, and started to cry. But he kept right on milking his cow. I knew he wasn't crying because I was hurt, but because he couldn't take any more problems. I felt that he was crying because I didn't get killed.

When the hay was ready for harvest Pa, Chic, and I would pitch in on the wagon and then lift it into the mow with a net-like sling. After every three or four loads some leveling off would be needed up in the mow. One day after working alone in the loft, I decided to descend from the mow by leaping to a hanging rope for a fast slide to the barn floor. Unfortunately, the rope was not attached topside, which in turn caused me to take about a twenty-foot fall to the wooden floor. No one was there to notice. I soon regained consciousness, and Pa ultimately returned to the barn with another load of hay. Pa announced that we had a couple more loads to go and all the hay would be in the barn. It looked like rain; so Pa was anxious to get the hay in the barn.

Our good neighbor who had once plowed our field offered Pa his new hay loader so we could finish our field before the approaching storm would soak the unharvested hay. The loader worked like a charm, much easier than pitching every fork full onto the wagon. On our trip to the barn with the last load, we kept the loader attached. This was the way it was normally done. But when we traversed the ditch area to get onto the old dirt road the load tipped. When the load tipped the hay fell off and the horses took off on a run for the barn, with the wagon and loader attached. Pa, Chic, and I were thrown in the ditch. Pa sprang up like a streak of lightning in order to ward off the horses from going through the gate between the road and the barn. I never saw anyone run so fast. He soon passed the horses and wagon. With wild swinging arms he got the horses to stop before they entered the gate. Pa then carefully walked the horses and wagon to the barn. The loader, still attached, survived.

Probably some of the most pleasant memories about work on the farm related to my cultivating the corn in the back field with one horse and single-horse cultivator. The corn would be knee to shoulder high. The horse and I would walk together row after row. About every half hour we both would rest under a large shade tree, where I would put my straw hat on the handle of the cultivator, give the horse a drink from a pail, and sip some cold water from a water jug. It was so beautifully quiet in the field, with birds singing and flying from tree to tree.

Another enjoyable task, though I didn't fully appreciate it at the time, was to watch the cattle along the sandy country road that ran along the side of our farm. Our sixty-acre farm was too small to feed the number of cattle, hogs, and horses that Pa had (about twenty cattle and six horses) so Pa would have the cattle graze along the side of the road. They were easy to watch for they were always concentrating on the available grass. I liked our cows; they were such gentle animals. Each one of them seemed like a personal friend.

Threshing was an exciting event. It was an annual activity on the farm where boys were treated as men and where neighboring farm men and women would render reciprocal help. The men would pitch the bundles of grain onto the wagons and into the threshing machine; the women would work together preparing the meal and feeding the men. The number of men on the job would generally be about twenty. Every farmer's wife would attempt to have the very best meal of the season when it was her turn to feed the crew. I took great pride in pitching the bundles into the threshing machine right alongside the other one or two men on the load.

A rather nasty event happened on one of the threshing days at a nearby farm. An owner and operator of a threshing machine decided his competitor should be stopped. During the night he managed to slip a steel rod into one of the bundles of wheat that was on the wagon adjacent to his competitor's thresher. The next day when his competitor got his tractor going and he engaged his thresher, the farmers climbed up onto the wagon and began to pitch in the bundles. It wasn't long before the bundle with the hidden rod was placed on the conveyor and into the separator. At this moment there was a loud breaking noise and the competitor's machine broke down. The culprit was caught and convicted. This brought on a dual problem for the offender: he was subject not only to the criminal laws of the state but to the disciplinary rules of the church as well. He ultimately had to stand up in the presence of the congregation of his church and confess his sin. If he would not have made such a confession, he would most likely have been excommunicated.

It was the generally accepted and required procedure in our church during those days that when a church member committed a sin that was public in nature, he would have to stand up in the congregation and publicly confess his wrongdoing.

The above-mentioned procedure was also required for young unmarried couples who became sexually involved and where pregnancy would ensue. Every now and then the congregation would get a surprise when so and so would be asked to stand and publicly confess their sin. I always felt sorry for the young people who had to go through such an ordeal.

My brother Chic never cared about the farm. He got a job in the city. But he lived at the farm, where he did some milking for his room and board. He often got me to milk his cows as well as my own when he wanted to go away. If it would happen that Chic would irritate me on an evening that he wanted to take off early, I would retaliate by not agreeing to milk his cows. On one occasion I remember being only four rows into the corn field when the expected call for me came from Chic. I wasn't about to answer. After repeated calls I heard him run to his car and drive out of the driveway. I raised my head above the corn to see where he was going. Just as I suspected, he was going to the neighbors to see if I as there. Back he came. Another series of calls. No answer. Chic had to milk his cows or get a temper kick from Pa. When he was done milking I nonchalantly appeared with a pail to milk the cows that were mine to milk. When I appeared Chic angrily inquired about my whereabouts. I said I was at the pond looking for some polliwogs. We however generally got along quite well.

Chic saved my life one day while on the farm. I was assigned the duty of rolling the east field with a heavy roller with no guards on it and with a temperamental unmatched pair of horses. All of sudden the horses began fighting with each other, and away we went, an uncontrolled runaway. I began yelling for help and holding onto the seat of the open roller with all my might. Chic heard me and saw us coming. He grabbed a long thin pole. As the team of horses galloped through the center of the building compound and toward the exit gate, he swung the pole straight across the head of the horses. They stopped and reared up into the air. I released my tight grasp on the sturdy metal seat, leaped to the ground and grabbed the reins. With my feet on the ground and Chic in front of the horses with a club, the horses diverted their attention from each other to the new threatening circumstances, which allowed us to bring them under our control.

The horses on the farm were a mixed breed with individual temperaments. They were a source of help, pleasure, and danger. My cousin Tom Reminga from Kalamazoo (son of my mother's brother Harry) learned about the danger of horses during a vacation stay at our farm when he was about seven years of age; I was about eleven.

Tom and I saddled up two of our horses for the purpose of giving a visiting school friend of mine a ride back to his home, which was about two miles from our farm. When we arrived at a distance of about one mile from the barn, Tom and I stared to challenge each other to a race. The race would start at the far end of a field that was along our route. With our uncontrolled enthusiasm we lined up beside each other. Then, hitting our horses with switches, away we went. Our horses were nose to nose all the way. Neither of us concentrated on stopping or slowing our horses as we approached the road where the race was supposed to terminate. As a result, the horses bolted across the sandy road into a wooded area consisting of thorny bushes and a swamp-like thicket. It felt like the thorns pierced every part of my body. I managed to get myself and my horse out of the brush area on to an open field next to the road, only to see Tom's horse galloping down the sandy road back toward home, with Tom's leg caught in the stirrup, and his head bouncing on the road about two inches from the horse's, rear hoof. Fortunately, the belly band on the saddle broke. Tom was left alive lying in shock and disbelief on the edge of the road that we had just previously traveled. The horse went back to the barn. My friend decided to walk the rest of the way back to his home. We returned to the house with a secret that was kept for many years. (It's ironical that years later I successfully represented the estate of Tom against the U.S. Government in a case where Tom was killed when a plane in which he was a passenger flew into a television tower guy wire in Wisconsin.)

I liked the animals on the farm. Most of them would always respond to love and affection. I had a good rapport with them, a much better rapport than I had with Pa. Pa never responded with any kind of love. I cannot remember his ever having complimented any of his children, except B, for anything they did. Nor can I ever recall his giving any affection to Ma. He was truly a non-responsive person when it came to saying thank you, or praising a child for having done a good job.

My sisters were not as fond of the animals as I was; they both harbored a certain amount of fear of them. Ethel was especially afraid of a large gander that we had on the farm. When she finished milking a cow, she would, as would each of us, take the pail of milk up to the milk house and put it in a ten-gallon can that was immersed in cold water in a concrete tank; water continuously flowed into this tank from the pump that was attached to the windmill. During this short trip from the barn to the milk house the gander would hiss at Ethel and then chase her. Sometimes the gander would catch her and attack her, whereupon she would yell for help. One day while being assaulted by the gander she fell, spilled her pail of milk, and hurt her leg. From that time on someone would generally accompany Ethel to the milk house. The gander was later eaten or sold.

Perhaps Pa was unable to affectionately respond to his family because he was hopelessly embedded in an economy that he could not cope with. He lacked education. He was losing money on the farm. He had five children, his last one permanently disabled and deformed. He was trying to run a farm and huckster produce in town. Northing seemed to work. Milk was ninety cents for a hundred pounds. The sugar beets in the field would cost more to grow than what the market would bring for the crop.

My uncle Neal (my mother's second-oldest brother) used to drive out from town to work in the sugar-beet field for a dollar a day. My brother, sisters, and I were also employed. We were to get paid when the sugar beets were sold.

During a hot summer day while the work crew were on their knees weeding the rows of sugar beets, Pa, who was a chain smoker, (he rolled his own Bull Durham) was standing next to the little milk house smoking a cigarette and watching us. After a few minutes of analytical observation Pa walked briskly to the location in the field where we were working. Upon arrival he got down on his knees and pulled weeds from between the beet plants at the fastest pace I had ever seen anyone perform such a task. After about two minutes he stood up and with utter exhaustion and anger, said, "There, that's how you weed sugar beets," and then walked disgustedly back toward the milk house. All of us became limp with laughter, perhaps in sheer relief for underneath all of this commotion was as a gnawing realization by everyone that there would be no profit in the beet crop.

Rainy days on the farm during the summertime were halcyon days. The pressure for everyone to work in the field was set aside by mother nature. It was a time when a growing boy could dream. I would generally retreat to the barn, where I would talk to the cows and horses. Occasionally I would crouch beside the udder of a cow and squirt some warm fresh milk directly into the mouths of cats. Sometimes some of my friends would show up for a game of tag in the upper part of the barn. But much of the time I would hang over the bottom half of a split barn door with a straw in my mouth and dream about some girlfriend and the possibility of some day owning a house of my own. I realized that the dream about the house was an unreachable goal. (I wrote this paragraph at our winter home, a condominium on the ocean in Boca Raton, Florida.)

Our farm, though small and profitless, was a place our kinfolk liked to visit. Sunday afternoons, after my sisters would return from young people's meeting at the church and just when all of us tired souls would attempt taking a little nap, we would often hear a car coming up the driveway. Someone would rush to the window and identify the incoming visitor, whereupon all the family would get up and greet the unexpected guests. They could not give us notice of their coming. We had no telephone.

Occasionally a friend of ours would come and stay at the farm for a few days. One such visitor was as a girl friend of my sisters. She used to live on the same street we did when we lived in the city. When it came time for lunch we all took a seat around our large round kitchen table. As usual, we all bowed our head in silent prayer. Pa never said a prayer aloud. When our heads were lifted, we began passing the food. My sister's friend took a slice of Ma's homemade bread and put both butter and peanut butter on it and began eating it. We all began to chuckle. Our visitor sensed that we were laughing at her. We all assured her that was not true. But our statements were false. None of our family were allowed to spread a slice of bread with both butter and peanut butter. When our guests broke the cardinal rule in the presence of Ma, and Ma couldn't do anything about I, it tickled us all. Ma was embarrassed by our conduct.

Our church and its "dominie" controlled our family's social life. We were required to attend the church services twice on Sunday. Later on, when I arrived at the young-adult age (16), I was also required to go to the young people's meeting. The main services were 1 1/2 hours long. They were held in the morning and afternoon during the winter months, and in the morning and evening during the summertime.

To ensure that each member of the church was being properly nurtured in the Christian faith, the church employed a person-to-person-contact arrangement known as "huisbezoek" (family visitation). The dominie and one elder would visit each and every family of the church at least once a year.

The announcement as to which families would be visited during a given week, and the expected time of the arrival of the church representatives, would be printed in the church bulletin. When our name would appear in the bulletin for this purpose, Ma would plan a house cleaning program that could be completed before the dominie's arrival. She would also make sure that she had enough food in the house so she could serve a proper lunch, which always included coffee and cake. In addition to being prepared within the house, it was clearly understood that the cows would have to be milked a little early on this day so everyone would have enough time to clean up and dress properly for the occasion.

About fifteen minutes before the estimated time of arrival one of the family members would be placed as a lookout for the dominie's car. Then the warning! Here they come! Everyone would get a bit tense. Ma and Pa would go to the door to greet them.

After a few handshakes and some mundane conversation, everyone would meander into the living room. The two best chairs were predetermined by Ma to be reserved for the dominie and the elder.

When everyone was settled down, the dominie would open the huisbezoek with prayer. The first few remarks or questions would deal with life in general. Soon the dominie would begin to probe each member of the family about his or her spiritual life. Was he or she growing in faith? Was worshiping on the Sabbath a meaningful experience?

In the midst of this type of questioning, Pa's face would begin to pucker and redden. Ma, noticing Pa, would get nervous. She knew what was about to happen. Pa would say something defensive and totally irrelevant to the conversation. Sure enough, Pa, in one instance, rocked forward in his chair and pointing his finger as if to make an important point, loudly said, "I Paul, the apostle, am the greatest of sinners!" Looking for comment from the dominie or elder, he settled back in the chair. Ma looked apologetic. We were all embarrassed by Pa's action. The dominie in an attempt to calm Pa said, "That's right

Andy, that's right. Paul said he was the greatest of sinners." Pa being satisfied that he made a point, and the dominie not really knowing what Pa meant by his emotional remark, the conversation returned to routine inquiry.

When the dominie was satisfied that he had performed his house visitation duties he would ask the elder to offer closing prayer.

Following the prayer, Ma would scurry into the kitchen and get the food. During this informal lunch a few jokes and kind words would be exchanged. After the lunch our visitors would leave, whereupon a great sigh of relief would be sounded by the entire family.

Following either the first or second worship service on Sundays, members of the congregation would generally invite some family over to their home for an evening visit. These visits were sometimes arranged a week or two in advance.

As a child I always looked forward to the Sunday evening visits with other families of the congregation. The entire family would usually be involved. This gave the kids of the respective families a chance to get better acquainted; it gave them an opportunity to play together. Hide and seek was always great entertainment. Sometimes we were even allowed to play cards, so long as we didn't use "devil cards." This meant we were essentially limited to the game of "rook." Checkers were also permitted. Theaters were taboo. Movie actors and actresses were presumed to be unchristian and bad examples to the young. They were people of the world. We were taught that we were in the world but not of the world, that we had to be a separate people. Dancing was exceptionally evil. The very thought of putting one's arm around a member of the opposite sex was in and by itself a sin.

Learning the doctrine of religion was mandatory for the children of the church. Catechism classes were used for this purpose. They were generally held on Saturdays. In preparation for attending these classes, I would get my rickety old bike out of the tool shed, put my white pet rat inside my shirt, and ride about 2 1/2 miles to the church, repeating the answers to the assigned questions until I arrived at class. Roll call was never neglected.

During class I would keep my rat on the inside of my shirt or overalls. I would hold my catechism book in a position that would conceal the presence of my little friend. Most of the kids knew that I had my rat in my shirt, but they would never tell the "dominie." We recited our answers cold turkey. Every student was asked every question. When the "dominie" would zero in on a particular student, my rat would get some attention from the rest of the class. The kids who had already been called on and were no longer mentally rehearsing their answers would intermittently glance at the area of my chest in order to keep track of the exact location of my pet. Deep down they were hoping that my rat would escape and create some real excitement.

One Sunday I was evidently a little too ill to attend the morning church service. On this same day Pa couldn't get his car started; so he and Ma went to church with Chic in his car. While they were in church and while my sisters, who for some reason were home caring for B and me, were sitting on the front porch, I slipped out the back door and went to see if I could start the family car.

Even though I was only about ten years of age, I managed to get the old car started. I got in the driver's seat, backed it out of the tool shed, and headed down the long driveway toward the road. That was my first lesson in driving a car. I taught myself. I made it out for the driveway and on the country road. A couple of minutes later, back up the driveway I came. I was surprised to see my sisters sitting on the porch. They looked very bewildered. Right then I knew I was going to get the poker across the behind from Ma when she arrived home from worshiping God.

On Sundays, one of my sisters and I would occasionally ride to church with Chic. Ma and Pa could, with this arrangement, come home right after the morning service. We were required to stay for Sunday school. One Sunday morning, after a light rain, Chic was driving us home at an exceptionally slow rate of speed. I chided him for going so slow. I said that I could run faster than the speed he was going. He bet me (without money — that was prohibited) that I couldn't run as fast as he was going. He stopped the car. I got out and commenced running. He went faster than he had been going and he never stopped. He went right on home — for a joke. I got so mad I intentionally stumbled into a puddle in the road , with my new trousers, and presented myself, when I got home, as an abandoned person who had gotten hurt in the race. Ma didn't know for sure whether I was, or was not, telling the truth, so she spared the poker.

Getting ready for the Sabbath required a great amount of work. On Saturdays all of the preliminaries were taken care of. Everyone took a bath. Ma and my sisters would wash and fix their hair. All basic preparations for the Sunday meal would be finalized; the potatoes would be peeled and put in a pan filled with cold water so they would not discolor, the meat would be placed in a Dutch oven and placed in the icebox, the green beans would be snapped, the bread would be baked, and all possible miscellaneous matters would be attended to . In addition to all of this, Ma would either do some shopping at the grocery store in Dutton or buy some necessaries from the traveling grocery truck. Pa would get the car filled with gas. On Sunday mornings we would milk the cows and feed the livestock. The family would then get ready for church in cramped quarters where there was no running water and only one outhouse. Ma would always appoint someone to stay with B. After all was accomplished, we relied on Pa's old car to take us to church.

One incident involving Pa's car is an event I shall never forget. Everyone was ready for church; so Pa and I went for the car, which was in the tool shed. Ma would generally come toward the automobile as soon as the car started. Pa, in an attempt to start the car, adjusted the spark and gas and gave the crank a few pulls; nothing happened. A little more adjustment of the spark was made. This time Pa spun the crank, still no luck. He made another slight adjustment of the spark, gas, and choke. Pa spun the crank again, then rested a minute. He said, "By golly that's funny," and I could see he was puffing hard and getting mad. Now with full determination he walked sharply to the front of the car, put his hand on the crank, and spun it as fast as a crank could turn.

No luck. Pa exploded. He yelled, hollered and screamed at the car. He kicked it on every corner and hit it with a club. The car still didn't go. At this point I saw Ma coming to meet us to find the cause for delay. She saw the ordeal. Without uttering a word and with full understanding of what was happening, she turned around and went straight back to the house. There would be no morning worship for anyone.

The old car had a reputation for running about 80% of the time when called upon to do so. When it did run, it generally went toward the town of Dutton. Because of this frequent direction of travel, and because the school known as the French Street School was also in this direction, and about a half mile closer to our farm, I was transferred from Holy Corners School to the French Street School. (French Street was the name of the country road that our farm was on.) I attended this school during my 7th and 8th grades. There were only two students in my class, Victor Olthouse and myself. I graduated with honors. I was the salutatorian; Vic was the valedictorian.

By the time I was in the 7th grade I was always looking for a ride to or from school. Quite often the county road commissioner would stop and give me a lift. I would always keep my ears attuned to the sound of an approaching car in hopes it would be the commissioner. If I thought it was his car, I would turn my head just a bit so I could determine whether it was he. I would never thumb a ride. I wouldn't even turn my head too far around when I knew he was approaching, for fear it would appear as if I was asking for a lift. Sometimes the commissioner would drive right on by me. When he would fail to stop I would regret not having turned my head around just a little more as sort of an encouragement for him to stop and offer me a ride.

My walk home from the French Street School was quite often interrupted by my desire to clean the cow-gutters in the barn of our neighbor, the township supervisor, who was responsible for my being transferred to the new school. He was a very busy man, and he always expressed great appreciation for my helping him with this distasteful chore. Sometimes he would give me a dime in addition to sincerely thanking me for help.

French Street School.

Things, however, didn't run too smoothly for me at French Street School. A change in classroom environment was not something I cherished. I arrived at the new school at an age when I had the capacity to be more effectively mischievous. A newly made acquaintance and I soon began to excite the other students with some tricks. For starters we obtained a board, just the right length, and put it between the bottom of the toilet seat inside the girls outhouse and the inner cross bar of the privy's only door. We then pulled the door shut, whereupon the board clicked under the cross-bar. This left the girls with no place to go. They had to walk to a neighboring house and get permission from the owners to use their outhouse.

During the winter a couple of us employed another ruse. My classmate "Vic" was, by design of the teacher, seated on one side of the room and I was placed on the other side. We were allowed to go back and forth occasionally to help each other with our study problems. When I would pass by the stove on return to my seat, I would insert a long, tightly rolled piece of paper in the back vent of the stove and inhale smoke. I would then push the paper into the stove pipe and hold the smoke in my mouth until I would reach my seat. When the teacher was distracted, I would blow a little cloud into the air. All the little kids would watch me and snicker. It was great fun.

My teacher finally caught on to what was happening. One day he set the trap. He acted as if he was distracted. As soon as I got back to my seat he asked me a question. I couldn't speak. He demanded an answer. He got it, filled with smoke. I had to stay after school.

Another episode involved my wanting a drink of water. I asked permission to go outside to the pump. Permission was denied. The window next to me was wide open. After a lapse of time, and when the teacher was busy writing on the board, I quietly slipped over the window sill and on to the ground. After I got myself a drink at the pump, I realized that I had to get back to my seat without being caught. I stood at the open front door entrance of the school house until the teacher turned his back toward the door. When I saw him edge toward the blackboard, I started nonchalantly and quietly toward my seat. The teacher unexpectedly turned around. I was caught dead in my tracks. The penalty for my misbehavior was another 30-minute stay after school.

When the school day was over, I slipped out and ran home through the fields in an attempt to avoid the penalty that was imposed upon me. The teacher decided to visit my parents at our home to talk to them about my misbehavior. I knew I was a solid candidate for a spanking from the teacher. I had had a few of them already. The teacher had a talk with me the next day when I returned to school. To my surprise, he assured me that he did not intend to spank me. He said that after visiting my home and talking with some downtown teachers he believed that the conditions at my home, which included special attention given to B, were probably part of the cause of my abnormal conduct.

During the last two years at this little country one-room schoolhouse I participated in what was known as the "Annual Field Day." All the small rural schools would meet at the local high school (seven miles away) for races and other competitive sports. I won the silver cup when I was in the eighth grade. That day was a day of mixed blessings. I wanted to wear my Sunday knee-length pants for the track meet, but Ma said absolutely not. I had a shine on a girl who would be at that meet, and, wanting to look my best at the field event, I sneaked my knickers from my bedroom. When I arrived at school, I changed from my blue jeans to my Sunday best. The last event was a high jump. I won the jump, but I cracked my ankle and tore my pants. I was taken home by a school representative. When I saw Ma, I was mighty glad I had a cracked ankle.

During this period of time, while still on the farm, Ma had a nervous breakdown. This was not because of me, although I'm sure I contributed to the cause of it. It was as a horrible experience for the whole family, especially for B, who would quiver when Ma would cry. While Pa was in the barn, and the rest of us were in the house, Ma began to tremble and cry helplessly. My sisters helped her into bed while I ran to get Pa. Ma was a very sensitive and kindly person. What she saw on the horizon for her own life and the life of her family was frightening. It was too much for her to handle. From this point on I began to understand more fully her repeated complaint that "a woman is nothing but a slave."

It was several days before she regained enough strength to resume some of her duties. When Ma was sick, little B would get terribly upset and concerned. There was a good feeling when Ma resumed baking bread and cooking meals.

During my years on the farm I was not fully aware of the financial and emotional trauma that was developing in our home. Pa and Ma were losing their farm. The farm equipment was breaking down, with no money for repair. The old automobile was unreliable. There was very little feed remaining for the livestock. Finally there was only one answer to the situation — an auction sale to pay their debts and to give the farm to the mortgage holder.

Knowing that his farm venture was doomed, Pa purchased a very small four-or-five case (12 quarts to a case) milk route from a friend for approximately one hundred dollars, which was to be paid for out of funds that were expected from the upcoming auction sale of the livestock and farm machinery.

Pa began this business by using the milk from his cattle and bottling the milk in the little milk house, the one where the cooling tank was located. The mini bottling plant was about the size of a small bedroom. The equipment consisted of a hand brush to wash the bottles, a funnel-like hand-held milk dispenser, and two small tubs to hold the wash water and the rinse water. The bottles were glass. The milk sold for six cents a quart.

In conjunction and in coordination with the purchase of this small dairy route, Pa made arrangements for a loan from Pete Wierenga, our grocer, to build a small processing plant, about the size of a two-stall garage, in Dutton next to Wierenga's store.

With the loan guaranteed, the date for the auction sale was set. The day of reckoning was now just a matter of time.

On the day of the auction everyone was up early. Pa and Ma were extremely tense. Their future survival was at stake. At the expected time of arrival the auctioneer and clerk (our neighbor) arrived for the purpose of making some pre-sale arrangements. In due time farmers came in their cars and wagons. They gathered in an area near the barn where the livestock and machinery would be sold. They all greeted each other with smiles and handshakes. Their conversations were generally about the hard economic times. Most of those present were feeling sorry for Ma and Pa. At the same time they were all hoping to buy something at a sacrificial price.

At the conclusion of the sale the auctioneer and clerk sat down with Pa and Ma to divide the spoils. The expression on their faces was grim. The monetary benefits of the sale were disheartening. Pa and Ma, after paying for the milk route, had only enough money for a couple of months' rent for an old house in Dutton.

Chapter IV.

Dutton

Home in Dutton where "B" died.

Shortly after the auction sale was completed, Ma and Pa collected their household furnishings and moved the family to the nearby town of Dutton. It was a small town with one main street and one back street. There were two grocery stores along with a grain elevator, the pickle factory where Pa sold his pickles, two gas stations, and two churches, one Christian Reformed and one United Brethren. This little community was rather lifeless, but it was three miles closer to Grand Rapids, where Pa and Ma had previously owned their own home. While they were now broke, Ma and Pa had memories of better days. Somehow they were re-energized with a determination to make a new start in life.

The house that we moved into was old, with creaky floors. There was no improvement in the toilet facilities. We still had an outhouse, and our baths still had to be taken in a wash tub. In order to bathe, each member of the family had to stand in a round tub, take a large sponge, soak it with water, and then hold it over his or her head and squeeze the sponge. Our baths were generally taken in the shed that was attached to the back of the kitchen. It got pretty cold in there at certain times of the year. This house, like our farm house, had a hand pump in the kitchen from which we obtained all our water. A wood-and-coal burning stove was used for cooking.

This eighteen-dollar-a-month rental home did have some good features. It had electricity. The family could now listen to gospel music and "Amos & Andy." (It was many years later that I learned that Amos & Andy were not black men, but white men, Freeman Gosden and Charles Correll.) It had a partial basement, an old clay bank "Michigan basement," but it was sufficient to have a furnace in it. The furnace at least gave the house some uniform temperature, which was a lot better than the old potbellied stove on the farm.

The house also had a living room that had its own door leading onto an outside front porch, as well as a sliding wood door that led into the adjoining family room. The family room, likewise, had a door that led onto the front porch. The living room, which was also called the parlor, was a sacred room. It was used on Sundays or when guests came to visit. The room would also be used when my sisters would practice on the piano. Ma gave them some lessons. Ma could play reasonably well for the limited amount of time she had to devote to music. Her favorite non-religious piece was the "Midnight Fire Alarm."

This old house was to be our domicile for the next few years. During this period of time it would be a place of turmoil, tension, laughter, and deep grief.

Living in this little town was a new experience for me. I lived in a large city until I was seven, then on a farm until I was fourteen. But I had never lived in a small town before moving to Dutton.

All five children were still at home when we moved to our new domicile. Dorothy was a teacher in a little nearby rural one-room school. Chic was working in Grand Rapids and was helping Pa, part-time, in trying to build a milk business. Ethel was working in town and helping Ma. I was in school. I worked part-time in Pa's new midget dairy after school, and full time during the summer months.

With the money Pa borrowed from Pete Wierenga, he built the proposed garage-like building. A boiler was installed in the building in order to produce steam to clean milk cans, to heat the building, and to heat the water for washing bottles. The building wasn't much, but it was a place to bottle the milk and store it in a home-built cooler. Pa successfully solicited new customers by contacting people who had purchased milk from him years before, people who wanted to buy cheap milk, and by servicing customers who wanted raw (unpasteurized) milk. Pa had no pasteurizer.

The milk route slowly grew in size, but the profits were near zero. Pa then decided to buy a few cows and milk them in the barn that was on the property. This brought plenty of work for all of us.

I soon became very active in peddling and bottling of the milk. In the summer months, when I was fifteen years of age, I was loading our one-half-ton panel truck with cases of milk at 1:00 am and peddling the milk to customers until approximately 8:30 a.m. I would then return home and help prepare the load for the next day.

This kind of work was very tiring for me as a fifteen year old, who was also active in sports. I was generally fatigued by the time the sun began to rise. One morning in the fall when we were still on the summer schedule, but when the weather was brisk, I fell asleep while driving the delivery truck and ran a stop sign. I collided with a competitor's milk truck. Our truck overturned on its side. The other truck was knocked against a pole. Milk was everywhere. Fortunately, no one was hurt..... I had heavy clothing on. My clothing was filled with glass, but I was not cut. Pa had no insurance, and he still owed the garage for just having overhauled the engine of the old truck.

With the kind of tension that was developing from an almost nonprofit business, there was no use thinking of trying to continue in school. I dropped out.

At this juncture Pa decided to sell the cows and buy all the milk needed for the routes from farmers. Instead of keeping and milking cows, he thought he would start a cattle auction in the old barn and withdraw from an active role in the milk business. Pa was the type that would get an idea for a business venture and then find himself incapable of handling it. He couldn't keep books, he was unable to write, and he was in a very real sense emotionally unable to manage any active business.

The cattle auction began in cramped space. A very capable auctioneer was employed to sell the livestock. Our township supervisor was employed as the clerk. Just before the first cow was to be auctioned, the gabby and extroverted auctioneer decided to give some flattering recognition to Pa for having started this great cattle sale. He yelled to the top of his voice "Andy! Where are you? There he is. Andy, get up here and give us a speech." Pa was totally squelched. But he had to do something. He reluctantly came up toward the auctioneer's stand. When he finally arrived and while still on the ground below the auction platform, he took off his straw hat, waived it in the air and hollered "Ya-hoo!" That was his speech. Chic and I were embarrassed to the core. We had a habit of laughing at our own blunders and the blunders of our family; so we made a quick exit from the crowd.

The sale was successful for a short period of time. But when a nearby auction with superior facilities opened in competition with Pa's auction, Pa's business began to falter. I was substituted as clerk, and a less expensive auctioneer took over. The auction finally closed.

During my months as a clerk at the auction I developed a skill for guessing the weight of cattle. I could guess the weight of a calf within five pounds of its actual weight. I also developed enough "know-how" about clerking to get myself a one-half-day-a-week clerking job at another auction a few years later while attending college.

Even though money was scarce, Ma and Pa would get to drive in to Grand Rapids on occasions. Sometimes they would borrow Chic's car, a 1928 Ford convertible, for the trip. Ma and Pa just had the milk truck and an old car.

It was always a big event to go to Grand Rapids to visit one of Ma and Pa's relatives. Something always happened that gave us a laugh. On our way home one day from Uncle Frank's house, (Pa's brother who lived at the bottom of Clyde Park hill) Ma nonchalantly waved hello to the people on the porch of the house at the foot of the hill. Ethel and I, who were in the rumble seat, wondered why Ma did that. Ethel said, "Ma, how come you waved?" This being our old neighborhood before moving to the farm, Ma said she was just waving at Mr. and Mrs. Quackelaar. Ethel started to laugh and said, "Ma, the Quackelaars moved from there at least two years ago." Realizing her blunder Ma began her uncontrollable sheepish laugh. Pa smiled; he never laughed with any vigor. But the two of us in the rumble seat, and little B who was in the middle of the front seat, kept right on laughing. All of a sudden Ma's teeth fell out of her mouth. This added fuel to the joke. Family blunders gave us our greatest fun. We had no problem laughing at our inadequacies.

Having to quit school, I turned more seriously to my job in the dairy. I was paid fifteen dollars per week, plus room and board. I was determined to build up the business. This I did. We soon had two trucks. My brother Chic took one, and I took the other. My route kept on building. Chic had a tendency to lose customers. A monthly adjustment was generally made; some of my customers would be transferred to his route. Chic was a respectable young man and a good guy, but he was not very aggressive. Perhaps it was because he suffered from having had three serious bouts with pneumonia when he was a boy.

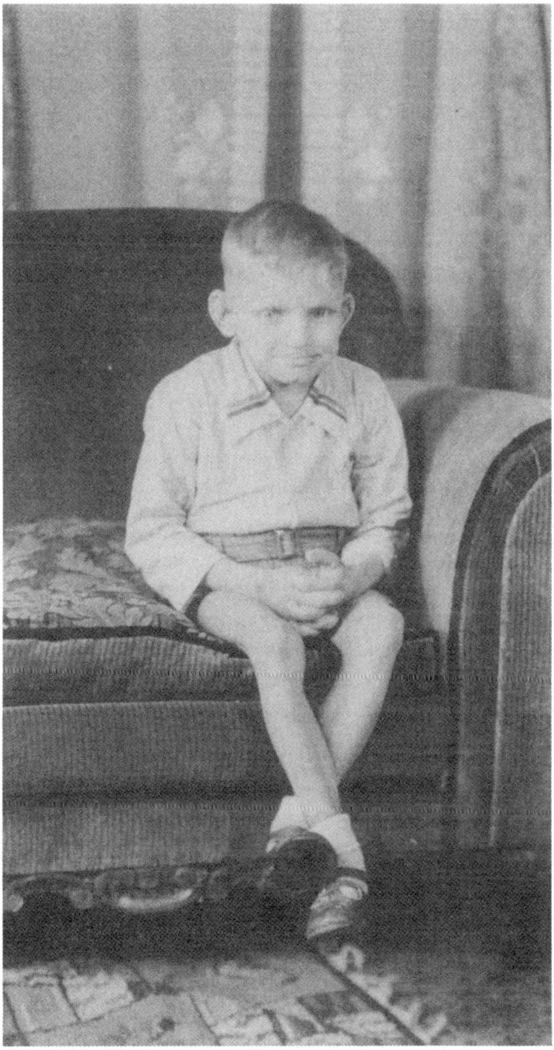

My brother "B" the year he died.

Chapter V.

The Passing Of A Saint

In the summer of 1936 little B was fourteen years of age. He never grew to be more than about three and a half feet tall. His little arms were small and atrophied. His legs were skin and bones. His hands were thick with calluses. He looked old for his age. The circulation in his hands was grossly restricted. At times he would totter over to the corner of the family room, lift up the corner of the rug, turn it back, and then rub his callused little hands on the corrugated backside of the carpet in order to get some circulation through his itching little fingers.

B's mind was good. He was very alert. But, as I stated before, his speech was restricted and he could communicate only with his family. He enjoyed sitting on the porch of our home in Dutton and watching the farmers bring in their pickle crop to the factory across the street. Occasionally a neighbor who would be walking by would stop and say hello to him. By this time in his life all his friends were adults. He could not realistically play with other children. His only little friend "Bobby" had outgrown him; and Bobby probably never even realized that he was B's only childhood friend.

During his time in Dutton B enjoyed, among other things, sitting on a chair next to my mother's sewing machine. He would talk to her and watch her with a great amount of interest. The closeness of these two was something to behold. It was the pure and undaunted and infinite love that existed between them that kept Ma's spirits high enough to endure the underlying pain that she daily experienced when she would reflect on the reality of B's deformity.

In June of the summer of 1935 B's health commenced to fail. He deteriorated rapidly. By the first of July, while everyone was getting ready to celebrate the 4th of July at the nearby Dutton Park, B's condition worsened. The family stayed close to home. On July 2nd the doctor came to the house and stayed . He knew the inevitable was about to happen. Fluid began entering B's lungs. In about five hours he was panting like an overheated dog. Most of the family were in the bedroom. Finally Ma could not be restrained; she lifted B out of the bed and held him in her arms. The doctor motioned to the family to let her be. She wept uncontrollably. Suddenly little B interrupted his breathing and in his own words quickly said, "Ah an go ge ga" (I want to go to Jesus). That was it. God granted his request. The saint was gone. When Ma realized he was dead, her weeping voice became a guttural cry. She sounded as if her very soul was being scourged. For several minutes no one could stop Ma from crying and no one could get the little body from her arms.

After the doctor got things under control, the undertaker came and removed B's body to prepare it for burial. The body was returned to the house the next day in a casket. It was placed in the parlor.

It was here that added punishment was given to Ma. Friends and relatives would come an say, "But Hazel, it's for the best." Best for whom, my mother would think. Her philosophy was that just being alive and loving each other constituted the ultimate in life on earth. Fragile and incapacitated as B was, he enjoyed his life, his family, and especially his mother. Now this love relationship was severed.

I can still see Ma sitting in the parlor near the casket on the 4th of July during the evening hours with sort of a paralyzed stare at her little boy. She appeared as if she had just returned from following B to the crossroad of eternity where she was rebuffed by God when she begged Him to let her keep her son a little longer. It was so silent in that room — sharp contrast to the distant sound of meaningless fireworks that were being displayed at the Dutton park.

The next day was the funeral. When they buried B, they buried part of Ma. Among those at the funeral was Uncle Dan. He viewed B's life as a tragedy and one that should have been exterminated by the medical profession at the time of birth. The very thought of anyone having such an opinion made Ma cringe. There was an obvious philosophical standoff between Ma and her brother on this issue.

After the funeral all the relatives and friends returned to the house, as was the custom in those days. Much visiting was done at this time among the relatives who had been separated by distance and time. When one of the friends or relatives decided to leave, it was time for everyone to say good-bye to each other by singing the song "God Be With You Till We Meet Again." This song generated teary eyes; they all realized that the next such gathering would be at the close of another person's life.

Ma never recovered from the loss of B. After his death she was much less inclined to laugh.

I, too, missed B after his death, but more so as the years passed by than immediately after his demise. With the benefit of time I was able to mentally catalogue virtues that were rightly his. I liked and admired what I saw. Little B was deprived of almost every activity yet he never complained. He suffered constantly with physical disability, but he was always cheerful. In a very real way he walked a laudatory path with a self-denying spirit. To me, B was the most effective minister I have ever known. Everyone who entered his presence left a better person than when he or she arrived.

Chapter VI.

A Personal Experience

The year of 1936 wasn't ready to leave without unloading additional burden upon our household. I had been plagued with strep throat for years. My tonsils had been a perpetual problem. Toward fall my tonsils practically closed my throat. The diagnosis was streptococcus poisoning. I was confined to the bed in Pa and Ma's room, the same room that was used to give special care to B. I had an extraordinarily high fever and was attended day and night by Ma and other members of the family. Grandma, Ma's mother, came to give some supplemental assistance. Notwithstanding all of this special care, my condition worsened. The doctor returned to our home late one evening. I heard Ma and Pa talking with him in the dining room with low-toned voices but could not hear what they were saying. After what seemed to be a lengthy conversation, they all came into the bedroom and together explained that the doctor was going to take some blood from Pa and inject it into my buttocks. After the blood was removed from Pa, the doctor rolled me over and put the longest needle I ever saw or felt straight into my rear. It was painful, to say the least. The next day my condition was no better. My strength was obviously fading.

When I was seemingly at my weakest I was informed that Uncle Harry from Kalamazoo and some other relatives were there to visit me. I could hardly respond. Their presence brought no encouragement to me. I knew they would be called only in an emergency situation. This frightened me. This fear was compounded when Pa got down on one knee at the foot of the bed where he said a silent prayer. I felt a little embarrassed, because Pa never paid any noticeable attention to me. It was out of character for him, and I assumed he was doing this for Ma.

The next few days were touch and go, but I finally began to recuperate. When I recovered sufficiently enough to leave the house, I was taken to a physician in Grandville, Michigan, to have my tonsils removed by a new diathermy method. This method consisted of inserting the tip of an electric needle onto the tonsil, after which the doctor would step on a peddle-switch, which in turn would send an electric current into the flesh. This would literally burn part of the tonsil. I underwent several of these treatments. I hated them. The smell of burned flesh, the resulting bad breath, and lingering soreness in my throat was something I shall not forget.

After regaining my strength, I decided to join a few other teenagers of our church in a pre-confession class. In this class we were given a relatively thorough overview of church doctrine as it was taught to us in catechism. It was more or less a review of the confession of faith set forth by the national synod that was held at Dordrecht in the years 1618 and 1619. In substance it stated that God is one in essence, yet distinguished in three persons, Father, Son, and Holy Spirit; that God created the earth and the universe out of nothing; that Jesus Christ is the Messiah; that because of the fall of Adam, man's representative, all persons need a redeemer; that this redeemer is Christ; that Christ died for our sins; and that because He is our redeemer and He did give the ultimate sacrifice we should profess our faith in Him as our savior and bind ourselves to the true church.

Upon completion of this class we were called before the consistory for examination. Each one of us was interrogated on the fundamental principles of faith. Not everyone knew all of the correct answers. One of our group, who was by no means an "A" student, was asked by an elder if after making confession of his faith he would be able to go through life without sinning. He replied in the affirmative; he thought he could make it through okay. With some correction from the consistory on this point and others, we were approved for the next step, the confession itself.

A few weeks later on a Sunday morning our group was ushered to the front row of our little country church. At the proper time the door at the front of the sanctuary opened, whereupon the dominie (minister) entered and proceeded to the pulpit. Approximately eight elders and deacons followed. They filed into a row of seats that was specially reserved for them during every service. The consistory was the guardian of the faith.

Dutton Christian Reformed Church.

Before the sermon and long prayer the dominie read from a form that was related to the act of profession of faith. He then asked us to arise and answer the following questions:

1. Do you acknowledge the doctrine contained in the Old and New Testaments and in the Articles of the Christian faith and taught here in this Christian Church to be the true and complete doctrine of salvation?

2. Have you resolved by the grace of God to adhere to this doctrine; to reject all heresies repugnant thereto

and to lead a new, godly life?

3. Will you submit to church government, and in case you should be come delinquent (which may God graciously forbid) to church discipline?

With the answer of yes to each of these questions we all became members of the church with the right to partake in communion.

My profession of faith became a corner stone in my life. But the mandatory restrictions that the church associated with the membership was unwarranted. In effect, it destroyed a good part of my youth. For example, we were not allowed to dance, or go to movies. On one occasion during my high school days five of us went to another town for a school-related activity. After our school activity was completed my companions wanted to attend a theater. I did not object to their going, but I was not allowed to go with them. I went to a restaurant while they went to the theater. As a result of these restrictions there was necessarily a limited rapport that I could attain with my peers. The regulations of the church were inhibitive.

After recovery from my illness I returned to my job in the dairy and on the milk route. I, however, decided that I wanted to return to school. At this juncture Pa tried to dissuade me from my decision to resume my education. His advice to me was the same as always, "Get a good job; its the best thing for a man to have." School to him, beyond the eighth grade, was an unnecessary luxury. But I was somehow determined to return to the classroom. I had no money to speak of, but with the work available to me in the dairy I could be worth my room and board at home and still go to school.

My return to school in the fall of 1936 was an uncomfortable experience. I was now in the in the 10th grade. I was also more cognizant than before of how different my religious customs were from the customs of the majority of students. I sensed, too, that the religious standard that I was bound by was not always appreciated by the teachers. The coach would sometimes make caustic remarks about the pious life style of the Christian Reformed people. This type of relationship with the teaching staff, along with my financial problems, made the school year rather rough.

It was also rather crowded during that year, living in the little new home that Pa had built on a nearby lot. With the help of Pete the grocer, Pa and Ma managed to get themselves back into a little home of their own. The house was very small, with only two undersized bedrooms. My sister Ethel was still at home. I therefore occupied the unfinished and uninsulated attic as a bedroom. It got mighty cold up there in the winter and terribly hot in the summer.

The house was built in a hurry by a carpenter who was a member of our church. He was so honest he insisted on deducting his coffee time from the hours he spent on the job. (Following World War II, and after I had made some money in the car business, I hired him to build some houses for me.)

When the school year ended, I had an employment problem. The young man whom Pa had employed to replace me wanted to continue working at his job. Pa at this time was entrenched, in a small way, in buying and selling livestock. He was known in those days as a "string butcher." He would travel in a truck from farm to farm throughout an approximate fifty-mile radius asking farmers if they had any cattle or other livestock for sale. If the farmer would have something to sell, Pa and the farmer would begin to "dicker" — to bargain with each other about the price that should be paid for the animal or animals involved in the sale. If they were able to get together on the price, the animal would be loaded on Pa's 1 1/2-ton truck, and off he'd go. He would either take his new find to another farmer who he knew wanted such an animal, or he would take it to a livestock auction where farmers and agents from meat processing plants would bid to purchase the animal.

Pa's truck was unique. Almost everyone in the farming community knew it. It had a large cattle rack on the back. On the front of the rack, on the top crossbar, he had a sign "Here come Andy." Pa didn't realize the word "come" should have an "s" on it. When Pa would drive his truck into a given area, it was not unusual to have someone jokingly say "Here come Andy."

Inasmuch as jobs were scarce, I decided to try to work with Pa. He said he would give me part of the profit on any livestock that I would find that was for sale. I worked at this job for the entire summer. This was not my kind of work. My net profit at the end of the summer was near zero. Pa also made relatively little profit.

My social life during the summer of 1937 consisted of swimming at Green Lake and Lake Michigan, going to the Volkema and Reminga reunions, participating in our local Fourth of July celebration, attending our annual church picnic, and getting together with my peers for various types of sports.

In addition to the activities mentioned, three of my friends and I decided to do something in music. Two of us could play mouth organs, one could play a guitar, and one could strum a couple of songs on a banjo. All of us could sing with limited abilities. After a few practice sessions we heard of a music contest for beginners at a nearby township fair; we boldly entered.

Following the performance of about a dozen entrants, our quartet was called to the stand. We did quite well. There were three of the several entrants who were recalled for a repeat performance in order for the judges to determine the winner. We were one of the three. We only knew the one song well enough to play in public; so we had to sing it again. The other two groups were more versatile. We didn't get the prize. That ended our musical career, although we did get together occasionally for our own enjoyment. One of our gathering places was the old run-down farm house of the Heyboer family. It was located a few miles west of Dutton. Mr. Heyboer, then a widower, was living there with a few of his unmarried children, including a mongoloid son, and with a married daughter and her family. Mr. and Mrs. Heyboer had raised twenty-two children, all their own.

In addition to being a friend of the Heyboer family, I became a very special friend of the mongoloid boy, whose name was Morris. Morris called me "Ruggs." When I would drive into the yard, Morris would be out of the house and hurrying toward my car before I could get the engine shut off. He would put his arm around me and lead me into the kitchen, where he would ask me if I would like some coffee. I always tried to remember Morris at Christmas time, even after I left the area. He liked large Christmas cards. (After I became an attorney I wrote the will for Mr. Heyboer which made special provisions for Morris.)

Chapter VII

Grandville

As fall approached, the subject of my returning to school began to surface. The financial problem had to again be solved, which in turn aggravated an existing incompatibility between Pa and me. This meant that if I were going to continue in school with any peace of mind I would have to make arrangements to pay my own way. I was convinced that a high-school education was a necessity. Therefore, I was determined to figure out a program whereby I could continue with my education. Ma thought as I did, but any expression on her part to this effect would only cause friction in the home. She could only impliedly approve of my going back to school.

My sister Dorothy was teaching in a one-room schoolhouse near Grandville, Michigan, in 1937. She heard of a farmer near Grandville High School who wanted to hire a young man to help him milk his cows. The pay would be one dollar a week plus room and board. If I could get the job, I would, of course, have to transfer from Caledonia High to Grandville High, which was about twenty-five miles from my home town. But this was an opportunity that would solve my dilemma. I applied for the job and was accepted.

The job was a disappointment. I didn't mind the work. I milked several cows each morning and night. I daily cleaned the gutters, picked up cow manure in the barnyard with a wheelbarrow, dumped it on top of a nearby pile, and worked all day every Saturday. However, the home environment at this new place of employment was a problem, and I was part of that problem. I always took a bath after work in the bathtub. At first I left a ring around the tub. I corrected this. Then the clothes that I wore in the barn smelled too bad. I guess I was too much work for the persnickety housewife.

Also I was causing too much expense for the stingy farmer. On Saturdays my sister Dorothy would generally make contact with me. On occasion she would let me use her Model "B" Ford. When she allowed me to use her car, I would show my appreciation by washing and cleaning it. After I had washed her car a couple of times, the farmer instructed me not to do it again, because they were hooked up to city water and they had to pay for the water.

I realized within a short period of time that things were not going to work out. The lady of the house was opposed to washing sheets and towels for an extra person, and the farmer was worried about an extra few cents that he was paying to have me there. My sister became aware of my predicament. She heard through her boyfriend about another farmer who wanted some help. I could keep going to the same high school if I would transfer to this new farm. The pay was the same.. The farm, however, was located three miles away from the school, and I would have to walk to get there; but I had no choice if I wanted to continue in school. I had to take the job.

When I arrived at this new farm, I was taken to my room on the third floor of the house. It was a finished attic-like room. The owner's daughter and her husband lived on the first floor. The owner and his wife, who were in their late sixties or early seventies, lived on the second floor. A stairway from the second-floor apartment led to my room on the third floor.

The name of these good folk was Glashower. They were immigrants from the Netherlands who spoke broken English. They were great and loving people.

I enjoyed my life at the Glashowers. The hours were long, and the three mile walk to and from school each day was no easy task. But the home environment was wholesome and pleasant.

The farm was an arm of the Glashower Dairy that was located in the nearby City of Grandville. I could relate to the total Glashower environment, having been raised on a farm and having worked in a dairy and on a dairy route. My job at this farm was milking approximately ten cows by hand every morning and evening, seven days a week, and helping in the fields on Saturdays.

I would be awakened every morning, including Saturdays and Sundays, at 4:30A.M., whereupon I would go to the barn across the country road and commence milking the cows. After I finished my assigned chores, Mr. Glashower and I would go up to his second-floor apartment and have breakfast, which was faithfully prepared by his wife. Prayer was always offered before and after the meal. Following breakfast I would change my clothes and wash thoroughly. I did my best to get the manure smell off of me before I would start for school. Just before I would leave for my three-mile walk, Mrs. Glashower would hand me my lunch, which ninety-nine percent of the time consisted of cheese sandwiches made with homemade bread. They were very good, but as I would gather to eat with some of my newly made friends at school they would jokingly bet on whether or not my sandwiches would contain cheese. Once in awhile I would swap one of these good "cheesers" with a friend for a different kind of sandwich.

My job and my transfer-student status at the new high school posed some problems. The job was so demanding that I could not possibly schedule any practice time for sports, and my being a transfer student disqualified me from playing on the school's team for a whole semester. My only participation in sports was during gym class. During this class the coach talked to me about the possibility of joining the varsity team as soon as the semester would end. But the varsity school rules and general economics ruled out any possibility of my being made a member of any school team during this first semester.

The long three-mile walk to and from school was pleasant. I walked part of the way with a couple of newly made friends. (Little did I realize at the time that one of these friends would be killed in battle during World War II.) Occasionally I would get a late start for school. This would necessitate my running part of the way. A few times I ran the entire three miles. At that stage of my life I was in good condition. I believe the cheese sandwiches were partly responsible for my physical excellence!

I learned a lot from this immigrant farmer during the time I was there. He would talk about world events, religion, business, health, languages, and many other subjects. Regarding languages, I can remember his saying that he could not understand the structure of the English language. For example, he said, "For the singular, the Americans say house; for the plural of house they say houses. But when they say mouse, for the plural of mouse they say mice." This system was unacceptable to Mr. Glashower. (He would generally say mouses instead of mice.)

My Saturdays in the field while on the Glashower farm were not devoid of fun. Pete, the son-in-law of Mr. and Mrs. Glashower, was an excellent corn husker. We would occasionally race to see who could husk the greater number of ears. On one occasion Pete said to me that he could husk corn faster than I could pick the ears up. He, in fact, bet me ten cents that he could husk corn in less time than I could retrieve them. I took this bet, notwithstanding it was against my religion to do so. The first few ears were easy. Time wise, I was definitely going to be the winner. All of a sudden Pete began throwing the ears in different directions. I lost the bet. Ten per cent of my weekly wage was lost due to a stupid wager. I deserved to lose. I wasn't supposed to bet.

After I had been at Grandville High School for almost a semester, the situation back home began to change. There was now a program available whereby I could stay at home, work part time in the dairy, and go to school. This would allow me to return to Caledonia High, where I had spent my first two years.

I left the Glashowers with mixed feelings. I enjoyed these good people. But by returning home I would not have to get up so early in the morning nor would I have to walk three miles to and from school. Instead, I would be riding about seven miles to school on a school bus.

Before leaving the Glashowers, I visited with them for a short while. During this visit Mr. Glashower told me how satisfied he was with my work and that he believed that I would be a great man some day. He said the last young man who worked for him became a doctor. I had no such goal. I just wanted to finish high school. Going to college was beyond my expectations. After some traditional handshakes I left for my parents' home in Dutton.

Chapter VIII.
Back To Caledonia High

I was apprehensive about moving back into my old environment. Pa and Ma did have a nice small new home. And Ethel was now married; so I could have one of the two little bedrooms. But whether I could psychologically readjust to being with my parents again was an unknown factor that had to be explored.

My return to Caledonia High School, now in the second half of the eleventh grade, again generated anxiety. I would be reunited with classmates whom I originally started with, who were now seniors, as well as with classmates whom I had joined after having dropped out for a year. Most of the same teachers were still at the school. There were a few new ones added to the staff.

Basketball season was in full swing when I returned. I was allowed to practice, but again I was caught in the school transfer rules. I was not allowed to play on a team for another semester, which was the remainder of the year.

There were a few intramural sports that I could participate in, such as wrestling and boxing. Our equipment at the school for these sports was sparse. But we made good use of what we had. I was a wiry, strong young man. No one my weight could beat me in wrestling, and only a couple of guys who were larger could overpower me in a boxing match. I also participated in the high-school glee club.

I cannot remember much about this second semester of my eleventh grade . I do recall that I was pleased to learn, toward the end of the school year, that I probably would be playing on the first teams of baseball, basketball, and football if I would return to Caledonia High for my senior year.

During the months following my completion of the eleventh grade I got a job selling lawn mowers, in addition to working part-time in the dairy. The mowers were rotary mowers. They were the first of their kind on the market. I sold several of them, some to the caretakers of cemeteries. The reel-type mowers were less efficient for the caretakers to use around the gravestones; they would not cut the buckthorn or tail weeds. The rotary mowers would. But I sold too many mowers, and my commission put me in a pay bracket above the accountant-manager of the business. The owner, because of this, wanted to put me on salary. This didn't interest me, and, as I was about ready to go back to school I arranged to work a short while longer and then readied myself for a return to Caledonia High.

My senior year was probably my most enjoyable year at school. I participated in most of the available sports. I was on the first teams of basketball, baseball, and football. I also ran in a couple of track meets.

Graduation day was finally scheduled. It was to be a happy occasion. I do not remember whether or not my parents attended, but there were forty-four graduates, and the small gym-auditorium was filled. The speaker addressed us with a timely message. The diplomas were handed to each graduate by the superintendent. I opened mine as soon as we were dismissed from the stage. My scroll was a blank. No warning was given to me as to why I would receive a blank diploma. I assumed the worst, that I had failed a subject and that I would have to somehow make it up. I went straight to the principal to find out what was wrong. She informed me that the key to my locker had not yet been turned in to the office. When this little matter was taken care of, I was given my diploma. With receipt of my certificate of graduation, I realized that I had finally reached my goal. I was finished with school. I was nineteen years of age.

Chapter IX.

College Bound

Having completed high school, I was ready to find a job. My brother-in-law, John, decided to leave the milk route and go to work as a mechanic for the Blue Arrow Trucking Company. The milk-peddling job was therefore available. I took up the route again, and by doing this I essentially ran Pa's part of the dairy. It was the same old routine, up in the morning at 1:00 a.m., then peddling milk from 1:30A.M. until approximately 8:30 a.m. Occasionally I would also help wash the bottles and bottle the milk in the dairy during the morning hours and during the evenings on Sunday.

Intermixed with all this work was dating, a head-on collision with an automobile I was driving, swimming, and ball playing.

It was during this 1939 summer that I went to watch my brother Chic's team play softball in Grand Rapids. The team, for some reason, was short a player. The pitcher suggested to my brother Chic that he ask me to play as a substitute. Chic was hesitant about doing this, presumably because I was his brother, but there was no one else available; so I was invited to play. I must have done well, for I was asked to join the team. This team became the league champions, and they remained the champions for five consecutive years. Softball was a game I thoroughly enjoyed. Fast-pitch softball (sometimes called diamond ball) was a sport that was popular at that time. Sizeable crowds usually attended the games.

As the summer grew short, I started to get an uneasy feeling about not going to college. Several of my friends had decided to continue their education. I didn't want to be left behind. But I was concerned about whether I was academically inclined enough to make the grade. I was sufficiently alert to realize that I would never know whether or not I could succeed if I never tried. I knew Pa would not favor my going to school. Ma would. Dorothy would also probably favor it. After a lot of discussion about the matter, I decided to enroll in Calvin College, our church college. It was close enough to drive back and forth every day, which allowed me to both work and attend the required classes.

College was tough for me. Working and trying to carry a full college course was next to impossible. In the warm weather months I would peddle the milk during the early morning hours, after which I would hustle to get to my 8:30 a.m. Latin class. It was in this class that I was most prone to doze. Needless to say, I did not do well in Latin. My professor once remarked in class that there are some students enrolled in college who work harder to go to school than they do in school. I guess I was one of those students.

My work schedule precluded my participating in any college sports other than those that were associated with gym, which was a required course. Gym was a course designed for the purpose of making sure the students got enough exercise. The school would not allow me to substitute the experience I got from peddling milk for the required gym work.

I did find some time to do some dating in college. It was exciting meeting new girls from various states who had a common heritage and similar interests. But finding sufficient time to date was a problem. In good weather I had to get home early so I could get a couple hours of sleep before starting on the route. Cutting the evening short with the college girls wasn't too bad, inasmuch as they were required to be in their dorms at an early hour, especially on week days.

There was one incident relating to dating while in college that I still remember. I became a friend of a classmate whose name was John; he was from Illinois or Indiana. He met a girl that he desperately wanted to take to a party which was scheduled for an evening during the week, but he had no transportation. He knew I had an automobile; so he invited me to go along on a double date. I declined, telling him that I had to get in early and that I had to peddle milk starting at 1:30 in the morning. John, in desperation, said, "Look, if you'll go on this double date with me, I'll help you peddle your route." I finally consented to go along, mostly because John was so anxious to date this new girl friend.

After the party was over and the girls were returned to their dormitory, a little late, we headed for my home in Dutton. By the time we got there, it was useless for us to try to get some sleep; so we loaded the truck and started peddling milk. After a couple of hours of running to and from houses, John asked how much longer it would be before we would be finished. I told him it would be after the sun is clearly visible in the sky. We continued on.

I had to pull at least one prank on John during this new venture of his. At one of the spookiest stops, where the milk had to be placed inside the back shed door in a semi-depressed area, I told John to walk slowly and be sort of quiet. The night was dark. I indicated that I would be delivering milk to a house on the opposite side of the street. What he did not know was that I would be present when he arrived at the back door. John delivered the milk inside the shed door, whereupon he turned to head back for the truck. As he stepped out of the shed, I made a weird guttural sound. John let out a yelp and raced to the truck. I slipped back to the truck from the other side and entered the truck as if I was returning from making my delivery to the customer across the street. He told me of his frightening experience. I doubted his story, but he insisted that it was true.

Shortly after daybreak we were not too far from the college dormitories, John urgently suggested that I drop him off, even though I had about another hour of work ahead. I complied with his request, and I finished the route alone.

When my work was finished, I changed my clothes and headed for class. The professor called the role. John was absent. In fact, John missed every one of his classes that day. John never again offered to help me peddle milk in exchange for having me drive him around on a date.

While some fear can be created in fun, some fear is well founded. One moonlit night as I was beginning my deliveries in my little home town of Dutton, I backed out of the front seat of the truck with a bottle of milk in my hand that I was to set on the doorstep of a local gas station. As I did this, a hand tapped me on my shoulder. I was scared, particularly because I had heard over the news that a hardened criminal, who was a brother of a local resident, had escaped from prison. I had been told that he was imprisoned for having killed his father and for having raped his mother. There was some local talk that this escapee might try to contact his sister, who lived in our little town.

This man who tapped me on the shoulder wanted a ride to the city. I didn't quarrel with him. I told him to get into the seat beside me. He did. I necessarily peddled a couple of cases of milk on the way into the more populated areas. The unwanted passenger repeatedly asked me if there had been any news about the Hendershot case. I said I didn't know what he was talking about. When I arrived at Wimpy's, an all-night hamburger restaurant in Godwin Heights, a city suburb, I suggested to my passenger that if he would unload the empty cases for me I would buy him breakfast. He agreed. I quickly went into the restaurant and told "Mom," the mother of the restaurant owner, who usually worked that night shift, about my suspicious helper and asked her to call the sheriff. She did. The sheriff came and took the man into custody. After interrogating him and holding him for about a day the sheriff's department let him loose. About a week later, the sheriff learned that this man was a co-escapee and an accomplice of Hendershot.

I was informed later that Hendershot himself was also in Dutton that night. A friend of mine caught a glimpse of him the same night I encountered his accomplice. My friend was parked near the local cemetery alongside the highway in his automobile with his girlfriend. Looking ahead he saw a man crossing the road on all fours. He concluded it was Hendershot heading for the house of his sister. My friend left immediately. The following day the youngest son of the escapee's sister was sitting at the door of a local repair shop. A resident of the area said to this little lad, "Hendershot was at your place last night, wasn't he?" The surprised child, who evidently was told to keep quiet about the matter, said "How did you know that?" (This little boy was murdered years later while serving a sentence in Jackson Prison.)

The combination of work and school was too much for me to cope with. I had to cut back. The next semester, as I remember it, I reduced my credit hours to the point where I could successfully handle the load.

Included in my new self-imposed scheduled was an opportunity offered by the government to take flying lessons for college credit. The only thing I had to do to get accepted into this program was to pass a physical and sign an affidavit which in effect stated that if the U.S. would ever get involved in a war I would fly as a military pilot. I took that deal. There would never be another war. World War I guaranteed us that.

Chapter X.

Military Service

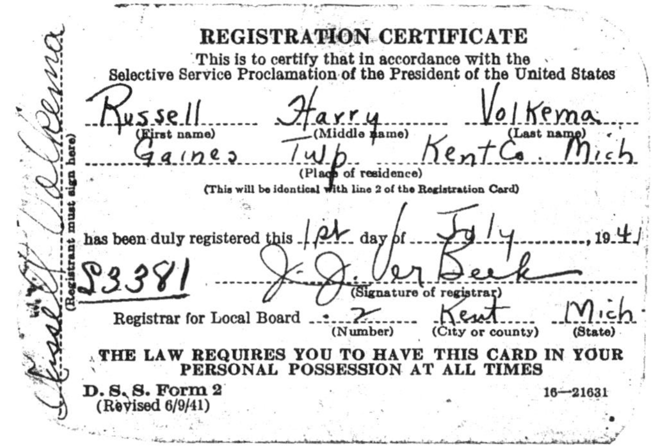
REGISTRATION CERTIFICATE

This is to certify that in accordance with the
Selective Service Proclamation of the President of the United States

Russell Harry Volkema
(First name) (Middle name) (Last name)

Gaines Twp Kent Co. Mich
(Place of residence)
(This will be identical with line 2 of the Registration Card)

has been duly registered this 1st day of July, 1941

S3381 J. J. VerBeek
(Signature of registrar)

Registrar for Local Board 2 Kent Mich.
(Number) (City or county) (State)

THE LAW REQUIRES YOU TO HAVE THIS CARD IN YOUR PERSONAL POSSESSION AT ALL TIMES

D. S. S. Form 2
(Revised 6/9/41) 16—21631

(Registrant must sign here) Russell H. Volkema

During the year 1941 I was still in charge of our small dairy business and attending college, taking a mini-curriculum. Part of this curriculum was the free pilot training course at the Grand Rapids airport. It was being sponsored by the Civil Aeronautics Administration, which at that time was under the Department of Commerce. My work in the dairy business consisted of peddling milk and overseeing certain responsibilities within Pa's very small processing plant. Other duties within the plant were handled by my brother Chic, who owned his own route. The bottling and pasteurizing of the milk was a joint venture.

Due to the deepening involvement of the United States in the European conflict with Germany, all young men between certain ages were required to register for military service. It was called "the draft." The draft was thought of as a mere formality. None of us would really have to serve in the military. I of course registered.

On September 8, 1941, I received, via U.S. mail, a notice that I was classified 1-A. This meant I was on top of the list of those to be drafted into service. On October 15, 1941, I was issued an order to report for induction into the army. This swift movement on the part of the government placed those of us who were involved in the dairy in a real quandary. I was the only person who really knew Pa's route, there was a shortage of available replacement help. I was still pursuing my pilot's license and I was attending college part time.

When the government sent me my notice for induction, it also informed me of my right to appeal. I appealed for a six-month deferment in order to complete my pilot's training, to finish my college courses, and for an opportunity to transfer the responsibilities of the dairy to some other person. My deferment was granted. After all, what was the hurry? There was no war.

Four months later, on December 7, at about 7:55A.M., the Japanese Naval Air Force attacked Pearl Harbor. This attack sank or damaged every American battleship in the area. These battleships reportedly represented almost half of the country's naval strength in that category. Other ships were lost, as were about 180 military aircraft and over 3,000 military personnel. All of this damage was inflicted by 105 Japanese carrier planes that slipped under the local relaxed peacetime American guard.

On December 8, at a little restaurant known as the "Bee Hive," near the college, I was eating a sandwich when President Roosevelt began to speak over the radio. In essence he said he did not want war but that war existed and that a declaration of war against Japan and German was the only avenue to eventual peace.

It hit me in the pit of my stomach. We were at war. I was 1-A. I was on a temporary deferment from the draft, and I had a duty under my pilot-training agreement to sign up with some branch of the Air Force. I kept my promise. I enlisted in the U.S. Naval Air Force as a cadet in February, 1942.

On the 23rd day of April, 1942, I received my orders to report to the Naval Air Training Base at Dallas, Texas. My semester at college and pilot's training course were by then completed. My private pilot's license was issued to me on March 16, 1942, and my replacement in the dairy was in place. I was ready to leave for military service.

At this particular time in my life I was dating a girl from another college who lived in a nearby town. Neither of us was of the mind that we were definitely meant for each other; but that possibility was there. After our final date before leaving for Dallas, I returned home to finalize some last-minute details before going to bed.

One of my unsolved problems was the fact that I did not have sufficient funds to get to Dallas. The government would give me a prepaid train transportation or it would pay mileage upon arrival at the base. I had a 1942 Ford convertible that I desperately wanted to take with me to Dallas. But I did not have enough money for gas. All my money was in the car.

I needed a hundred dollars for the trip. I assumed Pa would lend me this amount under the existing circumstances. But he was not inclined to do so. This was a low blow. After some argument, and a definite assurance from me that the government would reimburse me for my travel upon arrival and that I would immediately return this reimbursed money to Pa, Ma convinced Pa that he should lend me a hundred dollars. (I repaid Pa within a week after I arrived at the air base.) The next morning I started for Dallas via Kentucky.

I had no idea how far away Dallas was from Dutton. I knew approximately how many miles were involved, but, never having been on a long trip, I was not cognizant of the length of driving time that I would encounter.

While traveling through Kentucky I picked up a college student who was hitchhiking to his home in Paducah. As the day started drawing to a close, I began to look for a motel for myself. I would of course, let the hitchhiker try to hook another ride. When my student passenger realized my intentions to stop for the night, he stated that if I would continue on to Paducah I could stay at his home. I sensed his earnest desire for me to get him home, and I was short on money; so on we went, to Paducah.

When we arrived at my passenger's home, at about 11:00 p.m., we were both welcomed by his mother. She was a gracious person with a real Southern drawl. I could hardly understand her. The home was a typical middle-class Southern home. After some very pleasant conversation we all retired for the evening.

In the morning my passenger and his mother were up to see me off. They all insisted that I should have breakfast with them before leaving. We sat down around a large table that had been preset. At a certain point during the meal, when additional food was needed the mother called for the maid. Responding to the call was a heavyset black woman in a maid's uniform. I had never experienced this kind of social environment. I realized that I was appearing somewhat startled when the maid entered the room and was therefore somewhat uncomfortable. For the first time I sensed the reality of the division that existed between the races in the Southland, something that I was unaware of through experience. I had read about all of this in history books but I had never personally encountered such social separation. The only contact I had had with blacks was with a black neighbor who lived with his family in our farm community and who used to work for us on occasion. Whenever he would work through the noon hour at our place, he would usually have dinner with us. So this encounter with such obvious segregation was an eye opener for me, and an introduction to the Southland, where I would be spending the rest of the year.

After breakfast I gathered my belongings and prepared to leave. I shook the hands of my new friends, the student and his mother, and thanked them for their generous hospitality. They gave me their best wishes and asked me to send them my military address as soon as possible so they could write to me.

From Kentucky I drove south and west through farming areas, cities, and states. I observed firsthand the contrast between the beauty of the Southland and the extreme poverty within it, especially in the rural areas. Perhaps the greatest shock to me was reading signs over the drinking fountains which read "for whites only." I couldn't believe what I was reading.

Another "shocker" was the size of the farms in Texas. I had spent my boyhood days on a sixty-acre farm. In Texas a farm seemed as large as an ocean. Cattle and horses were there by the thousands. Not only were the farms large; the State of Texas was huge. I thought I was never going to get to Dallas.

Chapter XI.

Dallas Naval Air Base

Finally arriving at the Dallas Naval Air base, I drove up to the military entrance gate with much hesitancy. I was apprehensive about this new and uncertain life. After showing the guard my orders, I was told to park my car and was pointed to the building where I was to report.

When I presented my orders to the Officer in Charge, I was advised that all V-5 personnel were really Seamen 2nd class, and that they would retain that rating until they passed their basics. Then and then only, would the V-5'ers be classified as cadets.

For starters I was informed that there was no available military clothing. The base was short of the necessary garb for the incoming V-5 registrants. I was therefore instructed to continue wearing my civilian clothes and report to Barracks "B." Following these orders, I arrived at the barracks and found others there who also had not received any issue of military clothing.

The barracks was a long, wooden, two-story building with a locker assigned to each bunk. There was to be absolutely no talking after a certain hour. At the proper time I "turned in"; I was a lonely man among men, who after the light went out, inconspicuously said my regular nightly prayer.

The first morning at the base was an anxious one. The bugle sounded reveille. Everyone rolled out of his bunk, made his bed, dressed himself, and reported for muster. Following me to the muster area were others. Each and every late-comer squeezed to the left of me in the line-up. I was courteous and made a space for them. Finally the petty officer, a non-commissioned officer, hollered "Ten-Shun!" This definitely meant attention. After completing the roll call and giving a few instructions, he yelled "Right face!" I didn't know what "right face" meant, but everyone turned to the right and clicked his heels; so I did likewise — the best I could. Then came the command, "Forward march!" I had no trouble with that; that meant that I should go forward. All of the sudden the petty officer shouted "half left-hip." The other marchers started to bump into me. I didn't know there was a "half left." I immediately realized why the late-comers squeezed into the middle of the line-up. This made me one of the lead cadets. From that point on, until we got to the mess hall for breakfast, I was a nervous wreck. Not knowing any of the commands and being in a lead position where my awkwardness was magnified, I felt like a real dummy. I was wondering during this entire episode whether I would get washed out of the program before I even got my military clothing. That was the last time I was a lead man at the "E" Base (Elementary Base — also known as Elimination Base).

After breakfast all of the future cadets were escorted to indoctrination classes, where we were given an overview of the "E" base training course. Within a few days after my arrival I was issued my military clothing, after which I adjusted quite well to the routine of training.

Most of the cadets who were enlisted in the V-5 (aviation cadet) program had a college degree. Some of them had advanced degrees, such as law or a Ph.D. in some field of science. I had completed only two years of college, but I had one advantage over most of the others. I already knew how to fly. I was an inexperienced pilot, but I knew the basics.

I had difficulty in competing with the other students in two areas of the training programs, navigation and the Morse code. After making a special effort to learn the Morse code, I finally conquered it. But celestial navigation had me stumped. I believe I initially was the low man in my class; my roommate was at the top. This roommate was not a very personable individual. He had practically no friends on the base and was aloof and haughty by nature. But I got along with him quite well. I put some pressure on him to give me help with navigation. He reluctantly acceded to my request. Once he decided to assist me, he was thorough in his instruction. On my next examination I got a 100% (my roommate missed one or two of the questions and scored about 90%). When the scores were handed out I was asked to stand. I was designated as the person who made the most progress since the last exam. (Unfortunately this talented young man, who later became a pilot of a torpedo bomber, was killed during an attack on the Japanese fleet.)

The most embarrassing moment during my training at the "E" Base was not during the marching episode but in the classroom. The physics instructor made a few statements about aerodynamics and then questioned the class about the accuracy of his conclusion. Having some flying experience and knowing that his conclusion was erroneous, I raised my hand. When called upon by the instructor to comment on the accuracy of his conclusion I confidently stated, "I know that that isn't true." The instructor with enthusiasm admonished the class to be quiet and listen. Here is a man, he said, who "knows." I spurted out the basis for my statement and was 100% wrong. There ensued some real belly laughs from the other cadets, but this humiliating blunder made me several new friends. Since that experience I always state my thoughts in opinion form.

The physical aspects of my "E" base training was a breeze. I was in excellent physical shape. I could beat almost anyone over the obstacle course. The other calisthenics were no match for the exercise I daily encountered in the milk business.

While my training became routine at the "E" Base, it was nevertheless exciting and challenging, especially the flying. My flight training was in the N25, a biwing Stearman with open cockpits. The instructor occupied the front seat. The student occupied the rear seat. Both were held in by safety belts.

I well remember my first loop. I had had some training in aerobatics in a Piper Club, such as spins, but I had never been in a loop. The instructor thoroughly described the procedure and then entered the first phase of the maneuver with a dive. This was followed with a pull upward and then to an upside-down position. While in this inverted position I didn't rely on my safety belt; I grabbed a side bar for extra safety. I'd be lying if I said that I wasn't scared while in this position. I was greatly relieved when the loop was completed . It wasn't long before aerobatics became routine practice.

One of the toughest adjustments for me to make during my first month on duty was the confinement to the base. The cadets were not allowed to leave the base until they had completed the first phase of training; this took a month to six weeks. It was painful to see my convertible sitting there and not being able to drive it into Dallas. This frustration was compounded by a hail-storm in which the hail stones were as large as baseballs; they dented the total exterior of my car. The storm left hangars, planes, and automobiles totally demolished. My car looked like someone took a hammer to the trunk and hood.

Finally I was entitled to a pass. My intentions were to go into town, find a roller rink for Friday or Saturday night, and to attend a church on Sunday. Before leaving the base, I was given a tetanus shot. With this completed, I drove into town. I felt like a free man again. I checked in at the Baker Hotel, but after a few hours had elapsed I began to feel ill. I didn't realize it at the time, but I was having an adverse reaction to the tetanus shot. I became exceedingly sick, with a high fever and intermittent chills. The hotel doctor came to see me at my request, and I was literally confined to my hotel room for the entire weekend.

It was back to training on Monday morning. Soon thereafter I received word that I would be transferred each day by bus to an advanced training field. I was the first of my class (4B to be transferred. I was considerably ahead of the rest of the class in actual flight training, probably due to the fact that I had some previous flying experience. The CPT (Civilian Pilot Training Program) training I had while in college gave me a definite temporary advantage.

The cadet with the lowest rank at the advanced training base was required to carry the pails of human refuse from the temporary toilets to an area on the field and bury the stuff near a tree. Generally a cadet would only have a day of this. But by being ahead of the rest of my class in flight training I got the duty for well over a week. My cleaning barn gutters and stables during my farm days was a good conditioner for this most worthy task. My heart went out to the "fancy dancer" guys who were brought up in high society and who had to take their turn as a "honey dumper."

My new experiences at the advanced airfield were mostly pleasant, with some exceptions. On one of my solo flights I became disoriented. The cloud coverage was such that I lost my bearings in relation to the airfield. I saw a little log-cabin house in a field with two black people standing next to it. I thought I could safely land and take off in this field; so I landed, got out of the plane, and walked toward the little house to inquire about my whereabouts. The two black persons who were standing next to the cabin were women. As I approached the little cabin, they both went inside and shut the door. After a few knocks at the door they finally opened it — slightly. I asked them if they knew the direction to the naval air base. They knew, and responded by pointing.

When I chose the field to land my plane, I didn't realize that the grass was as high as it was. I hesitated in making a decision to take off from this field because of the long grass, but decided to give it a try. I just made it. The wheels of my plane touched the tops of the trees that were at the end of the field. I finally made it back to the base.

When I taxied into the line-up position after returning to the base, two members of the ground crew who were in charge of these planes were puzzled about the long grass on the landing gear. I thought this would mean a washout for sure if the facts were known to my superiors. I scurried away from the plane before any questions could be asked.

Fortunately for me, something had just taken place at the air base that overshadowed my error. My roommate was being instructed in an N3N, a forerunner of the Stearman, by an instructor who attempted to show my roommate how to do an inverted spin. This was a spin where the pilot is on the outside of the centrifical force rather than on the inside of it as is experienced by the pilot in a normal spin. Inverted spins were not allowed in the N3N. After the instructor got the N3N in an inverted spin, he couldn't get the plane out of the spin. He therefore parachuted to safety. My roommate had blacked out during this spin. When the instructor bailed out, it changed the center of gravity of the plane, which in turn allowed the plane to come out of the spin by itself. My roommate regained consciousness about five hundred feet above the ground, whereupon he took control of the plane and successfully landed it. All the concentration of the top brass and linemen was on the violation of this instructor. No one had time to examine the grass on the landing gear of my plane. Both my roommate and I felt very fortunate during the evening of that day.

When I reached the advanced state at the "E" Base, life became more pleasant. Weekends in this new and different city, making new friends, and receiving letters from friends and kin folk back home gave new impetus to my expanding life.

One of the churches I enjoyed attending in Dallas was a Methodist church. It had a special social program for military personnel and provided a great opportunity to meet new friends and enhance one's spiritual life. It was at this church that I began to experience the difference between the customs of the church that I was raised in and other churches. After the morning worship the young-mature-adult group would go to a nearby soda bar for refreshments. The young people of the church I belonged to back home would be highly criticized for engaging in such conduct; it was considered a sin to purchase anything on the Sabbath other than something necessary in case of an emergency. I did go with the group on occasion, but I felt uncomfortable in doing so.

After approximately four months at the Dallas "E" base I was given a certificate of completion and transfer orders to Corpus Christi, Texas. I was hoping for a leave to return home for a short visit before going to an advanced base, but no such luck. So I packed my few belongings, put them in the trunk of my dented convertible, and drove off, with another cadet, for a new phase of training. At this new air base I was to receive training in larger single-engine planes, and ultimately advanced training in PBY's, a twin engine flying patrol boat.

On my way to Corpus Christi I decided to make a stop in Shreveport, Louisiana, where our church was sponsoring a servicemen's home. The pastor of the Dutton church had been temporarily assigned here. After a pleasant overnight visit we headed for the naval base.

My cadet friend and I eventually arrived in Corpus Christi. Just around the gulf area was the naval air base, the future home for both of us for the next several months. The area surrounding the base and city, with its palm trees and coast line, was absolutely beautiful.

Corpus Naval Air Base, as I previously stated, was an advanced-training center. Included in the training program was instruction in how to fly larger aircraft; how to fly on instruments, and formation flying. The larger single-engine planes that were generally used were known as OS2U's and SNV's. Instruction in instrument and formation flying was given to us in these planes. I had relatively little difficulty in learning how to fly the "beam" and in learning how to control the aircraft in no-sight conditions. Formation flying was also easy for me to accomplish.

My advanced training at this base was in what was known as the "PBY," or Flying Boat. This was a little tougher for me to adjust to. The multiple engines, the clumsiness of the plane, and the landing on water procedure brought on a new challenge.

The flight instructor, along with a couple of students, would take off from the Bay and fly instruction patrol over a given area. We would practice landings and made practice bombing runs over a pre-set target. The target was a make-believe enemy submarine. In order to hit the target I, like the other students, was taught to take into consideration the speed of the aircraft, the direction of flight, and the direction and speed of the target. When the calculations were made and the plane was in the right position, the pilot would say over the intercom, "Bombs away." This would constitute an order for the cadet sitting in the rear of the plane to drop a small hand smoke bomb out of an open hatch, hopefully onto the target. We would then circle the target to see how successful we were in the bombing run.

I recall a thriller I had while acting as the bomb release man. The hatch that we would drop the bomb out of was toward the rear of the plane. As I was holding the little hand bomb ready for release, and without my parachute on, the pilot said, "Bombs away." At that very moment, as I was leaning out of the hatch to release the smoke bomb, the aircraft hit a down draft (air current) that put me in midair within the plane. I straightened my body out to avoid being thrown out of the hatch!

My last flight at Corpus was a flight test in the "ole" PBY-2. I had to fly it to the satisfaction of the check pilot. That test included take off, maneuvers in the sky, a couple of landings, and the ability to taxi the plane on water up to the ramp. I did only average on this test, but I passed. I was elated over this success. It meant that I had gone through my entire naval air training program without ever having failed a flight test. So far as I know, only two of us in our Corpus class, which included other "E" bases, managed to get completely through the flight training program without having failed a flight check.

Besides the flight instruction at the air base, routine training in calisthenics, marching, ground school, gunnery, and communication were all integral parts of the advanced program.

It was during a marching exercise at this base that I learned something about myself. After mustering and joining my platoon in a routine march I heard the petty officer shout at someone, "Hey you with the round shoulders!" Everyone of course kept on marching. He shouted again and much louder, "Hey you with the round shoulders!" I glanced at the cadence caller to see who in the world he was hollering at that wouldn't respond to him. When I made eye contact with him I realized he was looking straight at me. "Yeh, you! Straighten up those shoulders!" I couldn't believe it. No one had ever mentioned to me that I had slumpy shoulders. But he picked me out of the whole platoon. Realizing that I had a problem, I pushed my shoulders back and up and I walked like a tin soldier during the rest of the march. I certainly didn't want to flunk out of this officer's program after all of my training just because I happened to have slumpy shoulders.

Going into the city of Corpus Christi while stationed at this base was something all the cadets enjoyed. It was an interesting city. I cannot remember every staying off the base during my time at Corpus. This probably was due to the fact that there was a shortage of facilities in the city at that time. I do remember the drive along the bay. It was a breath-taking experience every time I drove into town.

One weekend I took a trip to San Antonio to see some hometown friends who had recently entered the Army Aviation Cadet Training Program. They were Pete Knott, Al Boss, and Henry Brink.

A humorous incident took place when I arrived at the gate of the army base where my friends were stationed. The navy cadet's summer uniform was white, identical to that of a naval officer except for the shoulder bar. The cadet's shoulder insignia was a small star without stripes. When I drove up to the entrance gate at the army base I received an immediate salute from the guard. I returned the salute. Unbeknownst to me the army security guard thought I was a naval officer with a rank equal to that of an army major. After having given me a salute, the guard answered my inquiry about the location of my friends, gave me another salute, and waived me on through. During my visit with my friends the duty guard evidently learned that I was not a commissioned officer. On my way out he stopped me, asked for my identification, and accused me of impersonating an officer. I of course denied such a charge. He claimed that I impersonated an officer by accepting his salute. I stated that I was merely being polite, that I accepted his salute as a gesture of friendship between the army and navy.

It was at the Corpus base where I met a person with my surname. I was in line for additional items of clothing where names were being called by the supply personnel. The name of Volkema was called. I stepped forward, as did a marine. We both made inquiry as to the name that was called. He said, "Volkema." I said that's my name. The marine said that was his name. It was Fred Volkema from Denver, Colorado. We were not relatives so far as we knew. But Fred was a member of the Christian Reformed Church. We met on a few occasions after that at a servicemen's Christian center in Corpus.

I attended several different churches while in Corpus; one was the Christian Church. It had communion every Sunday as part of its service. I had never heard of a church having weekly communion.

The people in the various churches that I attended were exceptionally friendly. Almost every Sunday someone would extend to me a dinner invitation; occasionally I would accept. I remember one of the invitations I accepted. About five servicemen were invited to the home of an elderly widow. Her home was a real show place. The dining room was truly elegant. Once we were all properly seated, a prayer was said. The food which was served was excellent, except for the side dish of crab. I had never heard of anyone eating crab meat. I had seen plenty of crabs around the mud holes near the barnyard, and I wasn't about to eat any crabs. I told this gracious hostess that crabs didn't agree with me. She was so surprised, saying she had never heard of anyone who was allergic to crab. I was embarrassed, but I was not going to eat any crabs.

In December, just before Christmas, the Navy notified me that I had satisfactorily completed my courses in flight training and that I would be graduating from the Naval University of the Air on the 24th day of December, 1942. I was about to get my wings and my commission. This was an exciting moment in my life.

Plans were made to drive home immediately after the upcoming graduation. I had several requests from other graduates for a ride northward. After the graduation ceremony all of the new officers received orders of transfer and a leave of absence. Four of us, along with our luggage, got in my convertible and drove homeward, from the moderate climate of Corpus to the wintry weather of Chicago, Illinois and Grand Rapids, Michigan. We were all anxious to get home; so we drove straight through, day and night.

Arriving in Chicago around 9:00 P.M., I called my girlfriend in Michigan and told her that I was on my way home. I informed her that I was fatigued from traveling but that I would like to stop in to see her for a short while if that would be all right with her. It was. She sounded very pleasant over the phone, but different. I was puzzled about why she wrote so often after I first entered military service but so seldom during the last couple of months. When I arrived I got the answer to my question. During my long absence she became acquainted with a fine young man with whom she became very serious. My stay was about an hour. It was obvious that this new relationship of hers was meaningful and something that had to be respected. I left for my home in Dutton, which was about twenty miles away. I had been gone for eight months and knew that it would be a good feeling to be in my own bed. I was the only child who still had roots in my parents' home. My two sisters and brother were married and had been living in their own homes for some time.

When I neared the little town of Dutton on this blustery wintry night, it felt like I was approaching hallowed ground. I had traveled over these roads so often with the milk truck, and for pleasure. Now they were carrying me back to my home after a world of experience. When I approached the driveway, the house looked much smaller than I remembered it. But it was home. When I drove into the yard, the house was dark, but when I got out of the car and slammed the door, a light went on. Ma got out of bed and greeted me at the door.

My meeting with Ma was a pleasant reunion. There were, however, no hugs or kisses. That type of relationship did not exist in our home. We sat up for an hour talking about some of the highlights of my training and about my girlfriend's new romance. I then retired for the night. Pa did not get up to say hello.

My stay at home was for a period of about two weeks. During this time I called some old girlfriends, went roller skating and bowling, and of course I attended church. During the war all servicemen were required to wear their uniforms. Dress uniforms were mandatory off the naval base. Although I felt a little overdressed for roller skating, I went anyway.

I was fairly good on roller skates. I kept up on my skating whenever I could during the months of military training. When I arrived at the most popular roller rink in Grand Rapids, with my new officer's uniform and wings, I was noticed by the rink supervisor. He chose me to lead what was then known as the "grand march." It was a lot of fun. I enjoyed skating.

While at the rink I met an old girlfriend. We went to a restaurant afterwards for a snack. While we were there, in walked my former girlfriend with her new boyfriend. I naturally said hello, and met her new beau. He seemed like a nice guy, and they appeared to be happy together. That was the night before I was to leave for my new assignment in Norfolk, Virginia.

Early the next morning I received a call from my ex-girlfriend. She was evidently having some reservations about her new relationship. When the conversation ended I suspected that her feelings were not all that solid for her new friend, but there was no time for additional calls. I was due at my new base within a period of time that required me to shove off. So I got in my cold convertible and headed east. My new assignment was to get additional training in a larger flying boat, the PBM.

The Colosseum Roller Rink 1943.

Chapter XII.

Norfolk Naval Base

I arrived at the naval base in Norfolk, Virginia, as an officer. It was different from my previous check-ins as a cadet; everyone was trying to help. I even began receiving bona fide salutes. The living quarters were also more pleasant than those previously assigned to me. But we never got to fly. There were only about nine PBM's for approximately five hundred new pilots.

While I was waiting for some flight time, my Uncle Frank (Pa's brother) died. I received a telegram from my mother to this effect. After showing it to the officer in charge, I was given leave to return home for the funeral. Here I had an opportunity to see almost all of my relatives on Pa's side. My leave, however, was for only a few days; so I immediately prepared for return to Virginia by train, the way I traveled home for this occasion. Ma and Pa took me to the train. I made it to the train just in time. After I boarded the train I turned around to waive good-bye. Ma was crying.

When I checked back in at the base, I learned that new orders were coming through for all of the excess pilots. I was called to the office after about two weeks. My new orders: To Olathe, Kansas, as a Primary Flight Instructor. While I was in a sense pleased at being chosen as a flight instructor, I was somewhat disappointed about not being able to fly the PBM's.

I made some new friends while in the Norfolk area, especially when I attended the Christian Reformed Servicemen's Home. (It was at this home where a picture was taken of me with a little daughter of the missionaries who were operating the home. About twenty-five years later this little girl, then a mother herself, moved to Columbus, Ohio , and joined our Columbus church. She surprised me one day by showing me a copy of this picture.) I would have liked to stay in Norfolk a little longer, but orders were orders; so back to the convertible and off to Kansas. A long trip was ahead. Little did I realize when I left the Norfolk area that back at the shipyard in Norfolk the Navy was completing a new aircraft carrier that would be my future home during some of the toughest fighting in the Pacific theater of war.

My trip helped me to appreciate the beauty of the Virginia and West Virginia mountains, the hills of Pennsylvania, and scenic lands of Ohio, Indiana, Missouri, and Kansas. But appreciation began to wear thin by the end of the journey. Then, finally, there it was, the Olathe Naval Air Base. Nothing spectacular.

Chapter XIII.

Olathe Naval Air Base

Checking in at Olathe was a pleasure. I was given excellent living quarters at the BOQ (Bachelor Officers' Quarters). Two officers to a room. There was a separate dining room for officers, and our rooms were attended by the cleaning crew.

I was at the base only a couple of days when I was sent to an instructor's indoctrination course. After this one-week course was completed, I was assigned certain students for instruction. I took my job seriously.

My work consisted of about four hours of flight instruction each day, along with some other miscellaneous duties. Like all flight instructors, I would work seven days and then have two days off. During these two days I would have access to any of the available NJ's or SNJ's for flight to wherever I would want to fly.

I had several experiences as an instructor that are presumably worthy of mention, if only to show you that a twist of fate would have spelled nonexistence for all of you.

On one occasion I was instructing my student how to land full-stall in a circle in a field, so I could relay to him the fundamentals for landing on a carrier. The student froze on the dual controls as we were coming in for a landing. We were in a bi-wing Stearman airplane, and he froze just shortly before the stall point. As a result, he stalled the plane about one hundred feet above the ground. This caused the nose to drop and allowed the propeller to dig in the ground while we were in a forward movement, causing the plane to do a forward somersault. We landed upside down right in the middle of the circle. I unleashed my safety belt, dropped to the ground, and got to the side in case of fire. My stunned student quickly summoned me, as he hung upside down in the open cockpit, saying, "Sir, would you please help me release my safety belt so I won't fall so hard?" I was already in motion to do just that, when I realized he was not releasing himself. Grabbing the release on his safety belt, I got him away from the plane as quickly as possible. Fortunately, there was no fire and no one was hurt. This incident brought me the distinction of being the only naval aviator who ever landed an airplane upside down in the middle of a target circle.

I had to make a determination whether or not to wash this student out of the program. Concluding that every cadet should be entitled to one upside-down landing, I let him continue. He did just fine throughout the rest of the course.

Another thriller came when one of my students was attempting to do a slow roll. A slow roll is a maneuver whereby the pilot, or student pilot, rolls the plane completely over on its back and then rolls it onward to its original level of flight; and this had to be done without losing too much altitude. This student was seemingly unable to do a slow roll. He did everything else well, but this he could not do. Unless he accomplished this maneuver, he would not be able to pass his flight check. I began to give a lot of special attention to this one phase of training; and after going through the maneuver several times with the student following through on the dual controls, I had him understanding that as the plane got in an inverted roll position he had to put considerable forward pressure on the control stick. (These N2N's had control sticks instead of a steering wheel.) I then turned the controls of the plane over to him completely, but only after doing a snap roll and a couple of other maneuvers in order to allow the student to start the slow roll from scratch. In other words, he now had to place the plane in level flight and then slowly roll it over and back to an upright position, in level flight, with little loss of altitude.

The student started into the maneuver with the acceptable standard procedure. As we approached the inverted position, I started to fall out of the plane. My safety belt had come unfastened during one of the preceding snap rolls. I instinctively grabbed the control stick to keep from falling. The student was not cognizant of what was happening in the front cockpit with the dual control stick. I realized that the student was trying his best to push the stick ahead but was unable to do so. The plane began a fast downward inverted decent. So I grabbed a side bar. This released my resistance on the control stick. By this time the student had so much forward pressure on the stick that when I let go of the front stick the dual control stick shot forward, putting upward pressure on the nose while in an inverted position. This threw my body partially out of the cockpit. As the plane rolled over, I was able to regain my upright position in the seat. I did have the required parachute on, but I had never jumped; so I was naturally deeply concerned about my precarious position while all of this was happening. I assured the student that it was not his fault. After we regained our senses, the student successfully completed the required maneuver. He later passed his flight check.

The next episode is a quickie. One of my students and I took off in an N2N (bi-wing Stearman) for a routine instruction. When we were about four hundred feet above ground, the propeller shaft broke. The engine kept on running, but it failed to turn the propeller. This cut the thrust and caused an immediate reduction in air speed. In as much as we were at takeoff speed, we were not much above the stalling point. If the plane would stall we would spin to the earth and crash. Upon hearing a slowing of wind passing the cockpit, I immediately pushed the stick forward and angled the plane sharply toward the ground. We headed directly for a creek in a very small field. Realizing this, I forced the plane to hit the earth just before we reached the creek, which in turn caused the plane to bounce over it. Then I ground looped the plane (putting pressure on only one brake) so it would not hit the fence. This was a job well done under the circumstances. The field was too small for take off after repair; so the plane was towed out of the field and back to the base. I was complimented by the base commander for quick thinking.

The incident that frightened me the most while stationed at Olathe was when my single-engine plane, an NJ1, malfunctioned during a nighttime cross country flight from Norman, Oklahoma, to Olathe, Kansas. The NJ1 was a two-person single-engine monoplane (single wing) with dual controls. The pilot in command occupied the front seat, whereas the passenger or co-pilot sat in the rear seat. As we were flying at about twelve thousand feet over a part of the country that was unknown to me, and which as very dark due to the wartime blackout regulations, the engine quit.

An engine failure posed a problem on this type of airplane. It has no self starter. It had to be cranked by a person standing on the wing. However, a propeller spin could be produced by means of a dive, after which the pilot would pull a lever on the inside of the cockpit and engage the starter. I tried this method. It was the only one available to me under the circumstances. It didn't work. I ordered the officer, a dentist, in the rear seat to jump. He sat there like a manikin. Again I dived the plane and pulled the starter. The engine again failed to start. I started out of the cockpit with the intention of jumping. I yelled, "Jump!" but there was still no movement on the part of the "Doc." We were now at an altitude that would limit me to one more try. If we would fail to jump after this try, we would be too low to parachute to safety. Also, I didn't know whether we were over hills, a forest, high-tension wires, or water. I gave it one last try. It caught! The engine started.

Just before the engine finally started, I had a peculiar experience. Within the period of a few seconds my whole life flashed before me — or within me. Things that I had long forgotten were made eminently clear.

When I landed the plane at Olathe about a half hour later, my arm was still shaking. As a result of this shaking, the plane repeatedly bounced up and down on the runway.

Getting out of the plane I asked "Doc," "Why in the world didn't you jump?" He said, "If you had jumped I'd have been right behind you." I gave a lot of thanks to the good Lord that night for allowing me to stay around a while longer. The NJ1, was soon put out of service by the navy. It was replaced by the reputable SNJ. The SNJ had a self starter within the cockpit!

I had another brush with death while still stationed at Olathe. On my days off, as I previously stated, the flight instructors could take the SNJ's or N2S's on personal trips. On one occasion I decided to fly home, and to land at the Grand Rapids Airport. I arrived there about midnight. As I was circling the field, my plane burst into flames. The tower observed it before I did, and the fire department was called before I got on my final approach. When I realized I was on fire, there was nothing to do but complete my landing. This I did. I shut the engine off and went in for a touch down. When the plane was almost stopped I jumped out of it and on to the runway, after which I scurried away from the plane. The fire department extinguished the blaze, and the plane was towed into the hanger for repairs.

When I reported the matter back to the base at Olathe, I was informed that another SNJ had caught on fire in midair over Tennessee. In that case the pilot bailed out and the plane crashed. It was later determined that some of these planes had defective carburetors installed in them which were supposedly the cause of the fires.

The routine activities of a flight instructor were never dull. An instructor would take a cadet, who may never have been in a plane before, and teach him the basics, aerobatics, night flying, and formation flying. Some instructors, myself included, would instruct students in inverted spins.

As I remember it, instruction in the inverted spin was not required but it was encouraged. This maneuver started as a loop. When the plane would reach the top of the loop in an inverted position the stick would be pushed forward, causing the nose to go up. The pilot's body would thereupon commence to fall out of the plane. He, however, would not fall out, due to his safety belt. The plane would soon lose its flying speed while inverted and would stall and spin toward the earth with the pilot being on the outside of the centrifugal force. This would force a rush of blood to the pilot's head and would also cause terrific pressure on the pilot's legs in the area of the safety belt. To recover from this maneuver, the pilot would have to react just the opposite of what was required of him in order to recover from a normal spin, where he would be on the inside of the centrifugal force. This maneuver was considered essential for fighter pilots who, while in a "dog fight," would climb after a target, and then concentrating on this target, would sometimes stall the plane into an inverted spin.

Night flying, which included landings on a grass strip in the field, was an eerie maneuver. For safety, there was a little light on the plane's wing tips and tail, but the grass landing strip in an outlying field was unlit, except for two little lanterns on the end of the strip where the planes were to touch down. This procedure with such minimal lighting was for the purpose of indoctrinating future carrier pilots, who would be guided by a few small landing lights to the deck of an aircraft carrier, where the flags of the landing-signal officer would bring them aboard. The lights on the carrier were designed to be viewed only at a low level so pilots of highflying enemy planes could not spot them.

On occasion the instructors would frolic around with the N2S's on their way back to the field after having given their students their required instruction. A friend of mine and I would sometimes fly with our wings interlocked. Smooth weather was required for this feat. Another "dilly" was to fly an inverted crossover. This would be accomplished by being higher than the other plane, entering a fast decent, leveling it off, rolling it over and then, as one approached the other plane, making a crossover to the other side. Then one would roll the plane to an upright position and fly formation on the opposite wing. We were criticized for this stunt and requested to discontinue it. We complied with our commander's request.

While at Olathe I would from time to time be visited by my old boyhood friend, Jake. He would travel to Kansas City from his army base in Missouri. On a couple of occasions I flew him back to his base. He came often because I had introduced him to a very attractive girl. This young girl became his wife after the war. (After Ma died this girl's mother, who was a widow, married Pa.)

Besides having contact with my old friend, I made many new friends while at Olathe, both on and off the base. There were two special Navy friends who would ride into Kansas City with me almost every time I went, except on Sundays, when I would attend church. Most of the time we would go our separate ways once we arrived in the city. We generally had dates. I was still interested in roller skating, although I didn't go skating very often. I also started to go to theaters. Up until this period in my life I cannot remember having attended any theaters. This was due to the strict prohibition against such entertainment by our church. Drinking of alcoholic beverages for me was also taboo. This principle was related more to my mother's personal conviction than to any instruction from the church, although we were taught by the minister that consuming alcoholic beverages was wrong. Ma's father and Pa's brother were alcoholics; so she was dead set against "drinking," fearing the result.

When my two friends and I would go into Kansas City with no special plans, we would generally stop at a large lounge in a hotel where servicemen and servicewomen would gather and socialize. If we would have separate plans for the evening, I would pick up the one friend at a designated place and then go to a certain hotel, where our other friend would be sitting in a chair next to the window, with his bottle of whiskey next to him. He never failed to thank us the next morning for seeing that he arrived safely back in his room. Our backgrounds were so very different (Irishman, Jew, and Hollander), but the chemistry among us was superb. I really enjoyed these two friends.

My Jewish friend, Chuck, got in some trouble with his roommate one night. We heard a lot of commotion in his room. Then we heard some belongings being set out in the hall. Both of these guys were good-sized men; so their reverberations were loud and clear. What was the trouble? Chuck's roommate borrowed some money from me one weekend. This left me without any funds to advance to Chuck as I frequently did. Chuck accused his roommate of tapping his reserve source of money supply. Though it had its serious moments, the incident became a real source of humor later on.

When I did start attending theaters with my dates, I suffered from a guilty conscience. Also I knew that I appeared rather ignorant. I knew none of the actors, not even the super stars. When I double dated with one of my friends and attended a theater, I commented as little as possible about the picture in order to hide my lack of knowledge.

My religion also prohibited dancing. Because of this I knew nothing about the art of dancing. One night I was asked to fill in at a party for another pilot who was assigned to night flying. I couldn't take his night flying, because we were allowed to fly only so many hours at night, and also the pilot had his own student for whom he was responsible. At least that is what I was told. Later I learned that there was some collusion in the deal. Anyway, one of the pilots was personally acquainted with some girls in a show that was coming to the city, about ten in number. He had arranged for his friends, including me, the substitute, to go with the girls. After dinner the music started. Everyone got up from the table as if someone had given them a command. They were on the floor before I could make an excuse to get out of there. With a great deal of embarrassment I had to tell my girl for the evening that I didn't know how to dance. I felt like a real dud, but my date was very gracious. She convinced me that I should give it a try. She pointed out that the dance floor was so crowded that no one would notice whether or not I could dance. I gave it a try. All the eyes of these devil friends of mine were watching me with chincy grins. I was the happiest guy in the would when the music stopped. My dancing partner said I did very well. She lied.

Besides some dating and getting involved in new social activities, I began receiving letters from my old girlfriend. She finally asked if I would like to have her come to Olathe for a short visit. I told her it would be great to see her again. She arrived by train and checked into a small family-run hotel in Olathe, near the air base. I introduced her to my friends. She stayed almost a week. The visit was very proper. I enjoyed showing her Kansas City and the air base. We also had dinner in the officers' dining room at the air base. However, the old chemistry between us had changed. Maybe it was because I had undergone intensive training and experience, or perhaps our respective attitudes toward life had changed. In any event, I had a wonderful week with a very fine and respectable person.

My health, while I was on the base, was generally good, except for a perpetual sore throat. The doctors' finally decided my tonsils had to be removed. I couldn't understand that, because I had had them burnt out with the diathermy method when I was in my teens. They finally convinced me that the physician did not get all of the tonsil; so under the knife I went, with a local anesthetic. After the operation I was taken to a hospital room in a very weakened condition. Shortly after I was placed in my bed, my throat began to bleed. The nurse was called. I was taken back to surgery. After a short examination I was taken back to the room. Shortly thereafter I began to bleed profusely. I had a hard time getting the nurse's attention, but when I did I was rushed back to surgery. Five doctors and two nurses were summoned. No one could find the trouble. The original surgeon said, "I believe we should put him under." I grabbed his arm and shook my head "no." I pointed to my throat indicting that he should go to work. Finally the doctor who was known as the drunk said, "there it is, let me take it." He did some suturing, and the bleeding stopped. When it was over I was limp. I was confined to the hospital for over a week.

Pa and Ma came to visit me. I think it was sometime following the surgery. They too came via train and they stayed at the same small hotel my girl friend had stayed at. I can't remember what we did together, but I'm confident that I showed them the air base and Kansas City. I also showed them my room at the BOQ. One thing I do remember. I took Ma and Pa to dinner at the Officers' dining room in the BOQ. The dinners were served at a long table with a table clothe over the entire length. We sat down alongside other officers, and there were other officers on the opposite side of the table facing us. I introduced Ma and Pa to the officers nearest to them. Ma and Pa were quite uneasy about being there. Ma was next to me, to my right. Pa was to the right of her. The food was served. It was pork chops. We began to eat. All of a sudden Pa picked up the pork chop and started eating it like one would eat a chicken leg at a picnic. Humiliated, I whispered to Ma to tell Pa to put his meat on the plate and cut it with his knife. This she did. Pa complied.

After a little over a year as a flight instructor, and flying off duty flights to Iowa, Missouri, Wisconsin, Colorado, and Michigan, my time, unknown to me, was coming to a close at Olathe, Kansas. My last off-duty flight was to Grand Rapids, Michigan. When I arrived back at the base, I was informed that I had orders for active duty on an aircraft carrier.

I had expected to be interviewed for sea duty by our commanding officer at Olathe, Dixie Kiefer. We understood that he was going to be the Captain of the new Yorktown aircraft carrier. He had been the executive officer of the old Yorktown, which was sunk during the battle of midway. My friend Gene was a friend of Commander Kiefer. He had been asked by the commander if he would like to go to sea with him. I understood that I was also going to be asked. But when the new Yorktown was ready, Commander Kiefer wasn't. His leg was still not healed. I was ordered to the U.S.S. Bougainville, a new baby aircraft carrier, which was located at Astoria, Oregon. My friend Gene was ordered to fly a transport plane between the Aleutians, from Seattle, Washington.

Chapter XIV.

En Route To The U.S.S. Bougainville

Having just returned from visiting home, and having but twenty days of leave and travel time available before arriving at my new assignment, I decided to go to Nogales, Mexico. If I had any conception of how long a trip I was to embark upon, I probably would never have made it.

I got my first glimpse of our Mexican neighbors after crossing the border. The poverty and substandard hygiene were appalling.. While there, I realized that I was never poor. The poverty that I was associated with was in a clean environment. Here my heart especially reached out to the little children who were suffering from disease and lack of care.

From Nogales I headed up through the California desert. At an army camp in the middle of the desert I paid an unexpected visit to my old double-dating friend "Epp." He was elated to see me. He immediately went to his commander and requested leave to accompany me to Los Angeles. After leave was granted, we got in my convertible and drove across the desert, relaying our military experiences to each other and revealing our hopes for the future. Even though it was a long trip through the flat and dusty land, it seemed like it took very little time before we arrived in Los Angeles. We spent two days there seeing the city and some of its highlights.

Following this short stay Epp boarded a bus back to camp, and I headed northward along the Pacific coast.

The California shoreline route was absolutely beautiful. The wide expanse of the deep blue ocean, the lashing of waves against huge rock formations, the long stretches of sandy beaches, the sea gulls flying through the sky, the tropical trees, and later the redwood forest, made the trip a breathtaking journey.

Upon reaching the redwood forest area, I drove into a park to observe the world's tallest tree. When I saw the height of it, I could not believe it. Standing next to the tree and looking upward, it appeared as if the top of it was touching the clouds. The tree was so large in circumference that I could not see the person who was on the opposite side of it. After viewing the tree, I went to a bench, where I sat and enjoyed the beauty of nature.

On leaving the forest area, I headed north. I began to reminisce and cautiously think of a future. Would there be much of a future? Where was I really headed? Did God have a plan for me? During this time, however, I had complete freedom as I traveled along, a freedom I knew would terminate upon my arrival at the naval base where I was to report.

Somewhere along the northern part of California (perhaps the lower part of Oregon) there was a sign pointing to a servicemen's club, a U.S.O. club I believe. Tired of driving and past time for an evening meal, I decided to stop and eat. The club was filled with army personnel and local civilians. Many of the civilians were young women.

I was there for only a few minutes when I realized I was somewhat of a novelty. I was the only navy man in the club. My naval officer's uniform (pilot's green gaberdine) seemed to be of interest to some of the girls who were present. While this embarrassed me in a way, I rather enjoyed the attention. Two girls who were sisters made a special effort to get acquainted with me. In the course of our conversation they said they were about to go home. They were going my way and wondered if they could have a ride. I presume gas rationing caused them to hitch a ride to and from the club, but I was flattered by their request and agreed to take them home. They invited me in when we arrived there, but I had to drive about another hundred miles in order to make the base on time. Reluctantly I declined their invitation.

During the last stretch of my trip, from northern California though Oregon, I began to tire. When I got overly fatigued I would get uptight, and my generally controlled manner would occasionally give way to Frisian-Dutch temper. As I was passing through a small city on a dismal day during this last part of my trip, trying to figure out the signs that would put me on the road that would lead me to the navy base, an irritable horn-blowing driver began trailing my car. After his blasting his horn at me repeatedly for about three blocks and at two different stop signs, my fuse blew. I stopped my car directly in front of his, walked briskly back to his car, opened his door, grabbed him by the collar, and told him if he honked his horn at me one more time I would knock his teeth out. He nervously apologized and agreed not to honk again.

I realized immediately after this confrontation that I was holding up several cars behind us. I particularly noticed an elderly couple directly behind the "honker." I slammed the honker's door, got back into my Chevrolet and headed for my next stop sign, which was about another block away. I was ashamed of myself. Pa had a temper like this. I determined not to let such a temper surface again and would sincerely pray about overcoming this dangerous shortcoming.

When I stopped at the next stop sign the elderly couple that had been behind the "honker" drove up beside me, on my left. They both clapped their hands showing their approval of my conduct. They probably had also been a victim of the "honker." Their applause made me feel as if my sin had been partially forgiven.

While the beauty of the state of Oregon was captivating and intriguing, my thoughts began to focus on my reporting in at the naval base and the uncertainty that lay ahead.

Coming upon the sign "City of Astoria" my long trip was at an end. After asking directions to the naval base from a local resident, I drove to the security gate for check-in. I was given permission to enter and was temporarily assigned to one of the nearby barracks. It was here that I met my future shipmates.

During the first part of March 1944, after being housed in the barracks for a couple of weeks, the personnel assigned to the U.S.S. Bougainville were ordered aboard ship.

Chapter XV.

Aboard The U.S.S. Bougainville

It was my understanding when I received my orders at Olathe, Kansas, that many of the seasoned flight instructors were being transferred to aircraft carriers as ship's personnel because they needed a certain percentage of pilots in the carrier air divisions. There were two main air divisions on the Bougainville: V-1, the flight deck, and V-2, the hangar deck. I was given charge of the V-2 division. This division dealt primarily with aircraft repair. I knew very little about aircraft repair. I reported aboard as a lieutenant, junior grade, commonly known as a lieutenant, j.g. Another pilot, a full lieutenant, was assigned to V-1. My assigned living quarters were toward the bow of the ship. My roommate was Jack O'Neil. Jack was a lawyer. My assistant was another lieutenant j.g., also an aviator, named Gerrish Gassaway.

The organization of the ship's personnel was soon complete. Stores (food, etc.) began coming aboard. All hands began to work at jobs they knew very little about. Everyone made an effort to get the ship ready for its maiden voyage. The ship itself was known as a baby carrier. But to a small-town boy like myself it seemed mighty big.

My new assignment was a challenge. I was an aviator given a non-flying job. Just a small-town young man who knew how to fly, I couldn't presume to know why I was assigned as a V-2 officer on an aircraft carrier. My attitude, however, was, I believe, constructive as I resigned myself to the task that was given me.

It took a few weeks before the ship would steam out to sea on a shakedown cruise. During this period of readiness all of the officers and enlisted men who were attached to the naval air corps wanted to log some flight time in order to get their flight pay, which was in addition to regular pay. I had the honor of flying the Captain of our ship as well as the Lt. Commander who was in charge of air operations.

My memory fails me as to just when we went on our first cruise, but we soon returned, having encountered some new experiences, some pleasant, some not so pleasant. I had been slightly nauseated most of the time, but on the positive side I got to take the helm of the ship on a few occasions and learned a great deal about how a ship really operates on the high seas.

When we arrived back in port, at Astoria, I was given orders to proceed to San Diego and report for training duty aboard the aircraft carrier Sergeant Bay. It was to be a seven-day cruise with extensive flight operations. Before reporting aboard the ship, I was housed in the Coronado Hotel in San Diego. Never before had I enjoyed such luxury.

During the second or third day out at sea on the Sergeant Bay one of the planes, during an attempted practice landing, stalled from too high an altitude. It bounced on the flight deck, missed the catch-cable and leaped over the safety barrier, right into the midst of a number of crewmen. Some of the crewmen were cut in pieces. Arms and legs were flying in all directions. Blood permeated the entire fore part of the flight deck. A young communications mate who was in the cat-walk at the port (left) side of the bow of the ship, went into complete shock. His eyes dilated, and his body became stiff as a board.

The remaining part of the training exercise was canceled. I returned to my hotel room and prepared for my return to Astoria, via United Air Lines. Just before leaving for the airport, I met a couple of personable "Waves" who were stationed in San Diego. I told them that if I ever returned to San Diego I would give them a call. After saying good-bye, I was driven in a navy jeep to the United Airlines ticket office, where my reservation was confirmed. I soon boarded the plane and was flown into Portland; from there I took a bus to Astoria. The bus trip was a ride through exotic country.

When I arrived back in Astoria, a small task awaited me. I was ordered to fly a small Piper Cub plane from Astoria to a military base toward the south central part of Oregon. A sunny day was chosen for the flight. The forests of Oregon were a beautiful sight, but the unending sight of nothing but trees made me somewhat apprehensive. There was no emergency landing area along my entire course of flight. If that little engine up front would have decided to quit, I had only tree tops as a landing field.

The flight, however, was uneventful, and I completed my task successfully and was then flown back to Astoria in a military plane.

In preparation for sea duty all members of the ship's company had to fill out an information form. One question required the naming of a certain person on board the ship to accompany his remains to his home town or city in the event of death. At this juncture I was thankful that I was by nature an optimist.

When the required administrative details were completed, our Captain was given orders to take the ship out to sea. After the cast-off was completed, we headed for the open waters. The members of my V-2 Division, like every other division, began to get acquainted with one another, with my assistant, Gerrish Gassaway, and with me. I set out to build a personal relationship with every man in my division. In addition to having good men in my division, I was fortunate to have a great roommate, Lt. Jack O'Neil. (We have remained lifelong friends.)

The Executive Officer of the U.S.S. Bougainville was a feisty little southerner. The V-1 Division Officer was also from the deep South. There was a real camaraderie between the two of them. From close observation of these two officers, my assistant, who was from the state of Delaware, and I suspected that both of them, especially the Executive Officer, harbored some deep resentment toward Yankees. Being from Michigan, I felt sort of uncomfortable in their presence; but, fortunately, the Captain of the ship was a considerate, nondiscriminatory, capable, and level-headed person.

On one occasion when I was in dress uniform and about to leave the ship, the feisty little Executive Officer walked briskly toward me and yelled an order for me to muster the members of my working crew who were assigned to load stores (goods and cargo). He then politely requested the V-1 Division

Officer to do the same. My Chief Petty Officer and my entire crew that was assigned to work duty were present and accounted for, except for one man who had been excused by the Chief Petty Officer. Only about one-half of the V-1 Division Officer's crew showed up for duty. The Executive Officer was obviously surprised. He appeared disappointed that my men were present and that the V-1 men were absent. He probably subconsciously assumed that the easygoing Yankee V-2 Division Officer was delinquent in his administrative duties. Anyway, I was vindicated, took leave, and went ashore.

While the ship was still in port, the entire crew was generally free to go into town during the evening hours. The U.S.O. and some of the churches were places the servicemen would frequently attend. The food was free. The bars in the area were also well attended.

Inasmuch as I was a committed teetotaler at the time, I would normally go into town with a couple of friends to the U.S.O. or to one of the churches' entertainment centers. Occasionally I would go to a bar with some friends. My drink would be a 7-Up or Coke. The price was generally the same whether I ordered a mixed drink or soda pop, but it was worth it not to have to drink the booze. I was determined not to be like my Uncle Peanuts (Pa's brother), who was an alcoholic.

There was a family in Astoria who were especially friendly to a couple of my friends and me. This family invited us on several occasions to their home for dinner. They were of Scandinavian descent. It seemed as if everyone there at the time had parents who had been citizens of either Norway or Sweden. The girls in the family were handsomely tall. They were clean-cut, personable, and polite and had a good sense of humor.

About the time my friends and I were getting acquainted in Astoria, we were informed that we would be shipping out. Members of this family who treated us so well made arrangements with a local garage man, a friend of theirs, to store my 1942 Chevrolet until after the war. I had also taken my electric shaver to a local drug store for repairs, but I was unable to redeem it before shipping out because the repairman had to send away for a part. He could not repair it before departure time; so I left the shaver there.

After several weeks at sea we put into port at San Francisco. My roommate Jack O'Niel invited me to go ashore with him, which I did.

Jack seemed to know something about San Francisco; so, when we got ashore, I just followed his suggestions as to where to go and what to do. This visit gave me an overview of the city and the experience of having dinner in a couple of very special restaurants.

I had the feeling when I was invited to accompany Jack into the city that something was bothering him. During this short stay in San Francisco I learned what that heavy burden was. Jack made a call to New York; it was to his aunt who had raised him from childhood. He was informed by his aunt that his marriage was ended, that his divorce was final. He was crushed. I couldn't really determine from the information I was given whether he was heartbroken because he lost his wife or because he felt he was a failure in marriage.

After staying the night in San Francisco, we reported back to the "Bougie" (U.S.S. Bougainville). We soon thereafter set sail for San Diego.

When we arrived in San Diego, I attended another one of our church's servicemen's homes. I also called one of the navy WAVES whom I had met in San Diego. She was an extroverted girl who seemingly had several friends. I suggested that we go out to dinner and that she should invite her girlfriend, whom I had also previously met, to accompany my roommate. They both agreed to go. My roommate's wounds of his broken marriage soon healed when he met this new and exciting young WAVE. (He later married her.)

By the time our ship arrived in San Diego it was time for me to get some flight hours in my log book. I had to accumulate four hours each month in order to retain flight proficiency and to qualify for flight pay.

My assistant, Gerrish Gassaway, also needed some flight time. We went to the local naval air base to get permission to use a couple of planes. The officer on duty said we could take a couple of SBD's which were dive bombers. I declined. I had not been checked out in the SBD. Neither had Gerrish, but he maintained that the planes were similar to the SNJ's and that there should be little difference between flying the SBD and the SNJ, a plane that we both were acquainted with. I disagreed.

I asked the officer on duty who the several SJN's on the line were assigned to. He replied that each one was assigned to a specific captain. I asked if he would be willing to give a couple of the captains a call and inquire whether Gerrish and I could use them to get our flight time, but he declined. I asked if he knew who the captains were and if he had their phone numbers. He had the phone numbers in the base directory. I took the names and numbers and called one of the captains and requested permission to use his plane in order to get my flight time. He willingly gave me permission to do so. He spoke to the duty officer confirming this permission. The plane was then mine to use.

Gerrish was not inclined to call one of the captains. He decided to take his chances with the SBD.

Before going to our respective planes, we had to determine which of our two passengers was going to fly with whom. One of my crew members, Edward Holistine, AMM 2nd Class, (a crew member of Gerrish) was a personable young man who was in need of some flying time. The other passenger was a fellow officer aboard our ship. Neither of them would choose between Gerrish and myself; they were too polite. So they flipped a nickel. The seaman, by means of the flip, was assigned to fly with me. The officer was to fly with Gerrish.

I started my plane, checked it out, and took off. As I was taxiing out, I noticed that Gerrish was indoctrinating himself with the SBD. I circled the airfield, waiting for him to get airborne. I thought I would join up with Gerrish and try some formation flying. Gerrish never made it. He was no more than airborne when his plane plummeted onto the runway and crashed. His plane exploded. I was shocked. I was hoping that it wasn't Gerrish, but a closer look from a low circling position removed all doubt as to whom it was that crashed. Both he and the officer were killed.

With the wreckage on the runway I could not land. I had to stay airborne for quite a while before I could return. It was a painful experience. My friend and my assistant, as well as the other reputable officer, would be sorely missed.

Upon my return to the ship I was notified by the Captain that I was the person Gerrish had designated to accompany his body to his home in the event of death. I was therefore given orders to do just that. I boarded the train which carried the body and casket. It was my task to see to it that it was unloaded in Washington, D.C., where it would be turned over to his father (who was remarried to a younger woman) and to his unmarried, divorced mother. His sister was also present when I arrived.

The internment was at Arlington Cemetery. At the proper time I presented the American flag to Gerrish's mother. After the funeral I was invited to the homes of both Gerrish's mother and father. Both of his parents, who lived in Wilmington, Delaware, were pleasant to visit with.

Mr. Gassaway, Gerrish's father, was the chairman of the Wilmington Chamber of Commerce. He was interested in knowing about the type of life that Gerrish and I had experienced aboard ship. He expressed his desire to know how I liked it aboard the U.S.S. Bougainville. I told him I liked the men aboard, with a few exceptions, but that as an aviator I would be more satisfied if I were in an air group or on a larger ship on the flight deck. He suggested that I go to Navy Headquarters in Washington D.C., and make an inquiry about the possibility of a transfer. I followed his advice.

When I arrived back in San Diego, and much to my surprise, I had orders to proceed to the U.S.S. Essex in the South Pacific. The Executive Officer of the "Bougie" seemed irked. My roommate expressed disappointment over my leaving but was pleased to know I was getting transferred to a more active ship. He helped me pack my gear.

Before I left the ship, I went to a place near the fantail to say good-bye to my men. Everyone there shook my hand. After the formalities, the crew handed me a picture of the U.S.S. Bougainville with all their signatures on the back. I still have that picture in my possession.

There was one of my crew members who was not at this meeting. He came aboard after we left Astoria. I was unable to gain a rapport with him during his short time aboard. But as I was about to leave the ship he approached me and apologized for being cantankerous. He stated that I made him realize that not all officers were S.O.B.'s. He wished me luck. I signed off, saluted the Duty Officer, and got permission to leave the ship. I was taken in a jeep to the train station, where I boarded the train for San Francisco.

Inspection- U.S.S. Bougainville- My division.

Chapter XVI.

En Route To The U.S.S. Essex

I cannot specifically remember boarding the train in San Diego for my trip to San Francisco, where I was to report for overseas shipment, but I do recall the ride.

The train was full, as were all trains between major cities during the war. I found a seat next to two Mexican-American women, a mother and her daughter. I had had very little encounter with Mexican-Americans. They all looked alike to me. I was not sure they could speak English when I slumped into the open seat. After several jerks of the train and several minutes after departure, some conversation commenced. The mother, as I remember, spoke English brokenly, but her daughter, who was about twenty or twenty-one years of age, spoke fluent English.

During our long train ride we got fairly well acquainted. In fact, when the mother snoozed off, her daughter managed to shift herself close to me. The trip was soon over, and before I realized it we were in San Francisco. The daughter and I made arrangements to have dinner together. The mother said she could not accompany us; so we went alone. The mother went to her hotel.

It was obvious during the course of our short date that this girl had some cultural training. We conversed extensively about her hometown environment, her family, and her ambitions. We also talked about my background, experiences, etc. The contrast between our respective upbringings was self evident. I was beginning to realize that I would have to relinquish some of my inbred customs and attitudes if I were to become a viable person. My subtle uncompromising criticism of the customs of others would have to cease.

The time came when I had to leave and check in with the commandant, pursuant to my orders. I took my new friend to the hotel where she and her mother were staying for the night, but before saying good-bye she requested my address, which I willingly gave her. I would not, however, be able to hear from her, or anyone, until I reported aboard the U.S.S. Essex.

While the checking in at the twelfth naval district in San Francisco was routine, my orders for the next leg of my journey were not. I was directed to board the largest known civilian flying plane, the Clipper, for a flight to Honolulu, Hawaii. It was a huge four-engine propeller flying seaplane known as the Boeing 314. Four of these planes were drafted into military service by the army, and five of them were drafted into the navy, but they were operated by civilian airline crews under contract with the military.

When I boarded the aircraft for my overseas flight, I wasn't sure the 314 could fly. There was one comforting thought I could carry with me: if there would be engine failure en route, the plane would at least have a ready landing area beneath us — the ocean.

It wasn't long after boarding the plane that the civilian plane captain gave orders to taxi out for take-off. On lift-off the engines sounded like roaring thunder. They were seemingly difficult to synchronize, i.e., to equalize the revolutions per minute on each engine. I believe the sun had already set before take-off; so the flight was essentially a night flight.

After the plane was airborne, almost everyone attempted to sleep; many could not. I was among those who felt rather unsettled. I guess I had experienced too many mechanical failures in airplanes to feel comfortable flying over this vast ocean during nighttime in this clumsy plane.

After a few hours of restlessness I decided to walk up toward the cockpit and ask the pilot if I could view the instrument panel. I had had advanced training in PBY's (twin-engine flying boats). I was interested in seeing how elaborate the instrument panel was on this giant plane compared to the PBY's that I used to fly.

When I arrived at the cockpit, there was only one pilot present. He was in the co-pilot's seat. I stated to him that I had flown PBY's and that I would appreciate it if he would allow me to review the instrument panel. He invited me to sit in the pilot's seat. After discussing the panel with the co-pilot at some length, I decided to take leave and return to the passenger area. At that moment the co-pilot, who turned out to be the third pilot, asked me if I would mind remaining in the seat until the captain or first co-pilot would return. He stated that both the captain and first co-pilot were taking a little snooze and that he was feeling uncomfortable with his assigned responsibilities. He also reluctantly confessed that he had washed out of the naval air training program. While he was in direct communication with the area where the other pilots were resting, he nevertheless had apprehensions about being alone. After about an hour or two the captain returned to his seat. I thanked him for allowing me to view the cockpit and returned to my seat in the passenger area.

A few more hours of flight and we were in Honolulu. We landed on the water at Pearl Harbor. I was taken to the local naval base, where I checked in and was given temporary living quarters.

I was assigned to one of the officers' barracks which housed both outgoing personnel and personnel who were returning from the battle zone. This new and strange environment called for some psychological adjustment. Many of the returning wounded servicemen had a frightening awesomeness about them. There would be instant silence with every new arrival of a single or double amputee. It was pathetic to see a one-armed servicemen, who had been right-handed, try to shave his face with a safety razor with his left hand. Shocking too were the wounded who suffered severe facial disfigurement.

I was informed upon my arrival that I would be staying in Honolulu for at least two weeks. This, I decided, would be a good time for me to visit the family of a Grand Rapids Japanese YMCA friend of mine, and to correct the scar on my forehead that seemed to be subject to a rash-like condition when I would wear protective gear.

My Japanese friend, whom I knew through YMCA activities that were connected with the sports program of Calvin College, had asked me if I would stop in and say hello to his parents and family in Honolulu if I every happened to be in that area. He had given me their home address and phone number. Little did either of us realize at the time that I would in fact fulfill this request.

Shortly after I was settled in my living quarters, I telephoned the number that had been given to me. A young girl answered. It was my friend's sister. I informed her that her brother had asked me to say hello to his parents and to his family. There was some hesitancy on the part of this young girl to talk. After a considerable amount of conversation between her and her parents she returned to the phone and invited me to dinner.

I followed the directions that were given to me over the phone and arrived on time for dinner. This was my first experience eating with a Japanese family. The home traditions, culture, and customs were almost totally oriental. The meal was served on a table, but everyone ate with chopsticks, although they were kind enough to give me a knife, fork, and spoon. I first tried their chopsticks, but they didn't work for me. I went back to the fork and spoon.

I didn't realize the pressure I was placing on these people with my presence. In the States relatives of the Hawaiian Japanese (Hawaii was not a state at that time) were being interned. Socializing with the Americans was evidently frowned upon by many of the Hawaiian-Japanese; however, the whole family were very gracious and courteous to me. We enjoyed each other.

When I was ready to leave, I was somewhat confused about the different corner on which I was to catch the bus back to the naval base. It was obvious to everyone that it would be a thoughtful gesture for one of the members of the family to walk a block or so with me to make sure that I would understand just where the bus stop was located. At this juncture one of the grown children confided in me that they would be seriously criticized and ostracized by several of their friends and neighbors if they were seen walking down the street with an American serviceman. Somehow I understood. Who was I to condemn these people? I found the bus stop with little difficulty. I rode back to the base with a somewhat broader view of life than I had before this unusual experience.

Dr. Sorenson, a medical officer from Davenport, Iowa, became a friend of mine while I was in Honolulu. I don't remember how we got acquainted, but he checked me into the navy hospital for a day and excised a small section of skin from the double scar area on my forehead that had been giving me some difficulty. All went well. While I was in the hospital, my doctor friend introduced me to a young personable and attractive navy nurse who had recently arrived from the States. We had a lot of fun kidding each other. She was from Kansas.

After my release from the hospital this young nurse and I saw each other practically every day until I left the area. We were rather excited about each other, and there appeared little doubt that we would resume this budding romance upon my return from combat duty.

During my stay at Pearl Harbor I flew Dr. Sorenson over and around the Islands. This gave me my flight time and it gave the doctor some entertainment. We developed a friendship that survived. I visited him in Davenport,

Iowa, after the war, and we also corresponded annually by means of Christmas cards and short letters. He is now deceased.

The time in Honolulu went fast. In October 1944 I was ordered aboard a navy transport plane and was flown to the war zone via several of the islands. I was placed aboard a tanker that was moored in the lagoon at the Ulithi Islands. I sat on this tanker for about a week before getting a glimpse of my new home to be, the U.S.S. Essex.

It was a boring time on board this tanker. All I did was get up in the morning, go to the mess hall for breakfast, and then go topside and look at the small islands and the several ships, including another nearby tanker. Finally, there it came, "the fightingest ship in the navy," the U.S.S. Essex. It was being escorted by destroyers, battleships, and aircraft. The ship was huge and almost mystical. It made the U.S.S. Bougainville look like a yacht.

The Boeing 314 Clipper.

Chapter XVII.

Aboard The U.S.S. Essex

As the Essex steamed into the area, the Captain of the tanker notified the Captain of the Essex of my presence on his ship and of my orders to serve aboard the Essex. A whale boat was sent for me. I jumped in and was taken directly to the boarding ladder of the Essex. I climbed the ladder, saluted the duty officer, stepped aboard, and then went up to the flight deck. As I reached the flight deck, the fuel tanker next to the one I was on was torpedoed. It blew up like a small atomic bomb. It had been attacked by a small one-man kamikaze submarine.

When the tanker blew, general quarters was sounded on ships in the area. U.S. destroyer escorts commenced dropping depth charges around the larger of the ships. The Essex immediately began moving out to sea. Just as the Essex was getting underway, bombs dropped in the ocean about three hundred feet along the starboard (right) side of the ship, from high-flying Japanese planes.

It was later determined that when the navy opened the nets for the ships to enter the Ulithi Lagoon the mini one-man Japanese kamikaze submarines sneaked in alongside of them. But why the navy failed to detect the approaching highflying bombers and why it failed to maintain adequate air cover for the carriers that were there, I'll never understand.

My situation was precarious. I had not yet been assigned to any room, station, or duty; nor had I been issued a life preserver or any flash-proof clothing. I therefore quickly descended to the forecastle (bow) on the deck below. Air cover for the ships was soon dispatched to ward off future air attacks. A period of readjustment and relative calm soon followed.

This was my first experience with real combat. I could not comprehend the fact that human beings were so determined to kill one another. Such inhumane conduct went against the very core of my being. Besides my religious or philosophical opposition to such conduct, I began to experience a degree of uncontrolled fear. Life on board this ship was going to be nothing like it was in Dutton.

After this rough initiation aboard the Essex I never doubted, nor did I have reason to doubt, that I, along with thousands of others, would be in the front line of combat in the South Pacific. And I realized that I was sitting on a bull's eye, a choice target, for Japanese bombers.

Within a short period of time I was given specific duties within the V-1 Division as an assistant flight deck officer. I was to be a flight dispatcher. I was also assigned certain duties within the catapult section. This would be my station during general quarters when I would not be dispatching planes. My personal living quarters was one-half of a stateroom. It was located just below the water line, torpedo alley, where enemy torpedoes would most likely strike. It was a place where prayer was intuitively appropriate before retiring for the night and where I faithfully and quietly addressed my Creator during my tour of combat duty. My petitions to God for physical and material benefits were, however, seemingly ineffectual.

At this juncture in my life I began to nurture a variance in my concept of prayer. I was experiencing no change in the nexus that is inherent in prayer, but the mode and expected results of prayer were being perceived differently. The formalized manner of praying became less important, whereas the impromptu approach became more significant. In essence, I adopted as more meaningful the mode of prayer that is set forth in the old hymn by James Montgomery and Bates G. Burt where "prayer is the soul's sincere desire, unuttered or expressed the burden of a sigh, the falling of a tear, and the upward glancing of the eye."

While the petitioning mode of prayer was, for me, expanding, the expected response became more restricted. A frantic appeal to God that no one would be hurt during battle would not curb the onslaught of death and destruction. I did feel, however, that I was experiencing a response to whatever it was that was related to the well-being of my soul and conscience. I felt an assurance that God was protecting the essence of my spiritual being, that no matter what would happen to me, the lifelike image of God that is contained within my soul would not be destroyed.

The bottom line of my adjusted concept of prayer at that time was that God could transcend His created order of things and miraculously alter the physical and material elements of nature, and that He did in fact do this in the earth's early formative years; but that for the sake of consistency and stability, He no longer would disrupt this order by intervention. I was unable to see any change in the physical or material aspects of creation that could not be explained within the confines of the natural order of things. God did, however, seemingly respond to a petitionary prayer as it would relate to the petitioner's soul. He, I concluded, will not forsake this element of the finite, regardless of any surrounding adverse circumstances.

I was not too satisfied with my new assignment on the Essex and had a difficult time accepting another non-flying position. When the Essex would retreat to a relatively safe area where the damaged planes would be flown off the carrier to an island, I would get a plane and fly it in order to log some flight time. During such flights I would fly patrol, but my primary duty aboard the Essex did not involve flying. My duties required me to direct each plane into a certain position on the flight deck, have the pilot rev up the engine, determine whether the engine was performing properly, observe the upswing of the bow of the ship, and then, just before the bow would start upward, signal to the pilot to take off. Also within my duties was the responsibility of catapulting aircraft. If the wind was slow, we would keep catapulting planes until there was enough takeoff distance on the flight deck for the remaining planes to fly off on their own power.

It was during the course of dispatching planes that I realized that it would be better if all the planes were to leave the flight deck at an angle, so they would fly off the front starboard (right) corner. This, in my opinion, was a much safer procedure. The ship itself was always turned into the wind before launching, with a three-degree crosswind toward the starboard side. With the procedure being used, when the departing plane would fly straight ahead, its slip-stream would remain in its wake for a few seconds, which in turn would delay the next takeoff. Also, if the departing plane would have a power failure it would most likely land in the water directly in the path of the ship and be run over by the ship and sunk.

I therefore started to cock the planes toward the starboard corner of the bow before directing the pilot to rev up the engine in preparation for takeoff. When the bow of the ship would hit the bottom of a dip and start upward I would give him the signal to go. This worked well. As soon as the plane left the ship, the plane would be off to the starboard side of the ship. The forward movement of the ship would, at that instance, be beyond the slipstream of the departing aircraft. This meant that as soon as the tail of the departing plane left the deck I was free to signal the next one in line to follow suit.

At first I got some flack from the officers on the bridge. They did not appreciate the unorthodox dispatching procedure. But their criticism was soon muted by the compliments the Essex would receive from the admiral who was generally aboard a nearby sister ship. The Essex would receive messages such as "an excellent launch" or "keep up the good work," etc.

During the initial and experimental change in this dispatching technique the Essex would generally launch its planes in less time than the other participating carriers. To my knowledge this was the beginning of the angle takeoff from carriers.

Little did I realize when I reported aboard the Essex how extensive my participation would be in actual combat. I ultimately served in five major engagements. Each major engagement involved several battles. The actions which the U.S.S. Essex took part in while I was aboard are set forth in the U.S. Naval records. They are as follows:

Raid on Manila, 5-6 Nov., 1944.
Raid on Ormoc Bay Shipping, 11 Nov., 1944.
Raid on Manila, 13-14 Nov., 1944.
Raid on Manila, 25 Nov., 1944.
Invasion of Mindoro, 14-16 Dec., 1944.
Raid on Formosa and Okinawa Jima, 3-4 Jan., 1945.
Raid on Northern Luzon, 6-7 Jan., 1945.
Raid on Formosa, Miyako Jima and Okinawa Jima, 9 Jan., 1945.
Raid on Camranh Bay, Cape St. Jacques, and Saigon, French Indo China, 12 Jan., 1945.
Raid on Swatow and Formosa, 15 Jan., 1945.
Raid on Hainan and Hong Kong, 16 Jan., 1945.
Raid on Formosa and Saki Shima Gunto, 21 Jan., 1945.
Raid on Okinawa Gunto, 22 Jan., 1945.
Raid on Tokyo, 16-17 Feb., 1945.
Invasion of Iow Jima, 19 Feb., 1945.
Raid on Iwo Jim, Haha Jima, and Chichi Jima, 21 Feb., 1945.

Raid on Tokyo, 25 Feb., 1945.
Raid on Okinawa Jima, 1 Mar., 1945.
Raid on Hyushu, 18 Mar., 1945.
Raid on Fleet Units of Kure, 19 Mar., 1945.
Raid on Okinawa Jima, 23-24 Mar., 1945.
Raid on Okinawa Jima, 26-27 Mar., 1945.
Raid on Kyushu, 29 Mar., 1945.
Invasion of Kermama Retto, 30-3 Mar., 1945.
Invasion of Okinawa Jima, 1 Apr., 1945.
Raid on Ie Shima, 3-4 Apr. 1945.,
Raid on Kikai Shima, 5 Apr., 1945.
Annihilation of Yamoto Task Group, 7 Apr., 1945.
Raid on Okinawa Jima, 8 Apr., 1945.
Support Missions for Okinawa Jima Invasion Forces, 11-13 Apr., 1945.
Support Missions for Okinawa Jima Invasion Forces, 15-17 Apr., 1945.
Support Missions for Okinawa Jima Invasion Forces, 19-22 Apr., 1945.
Support Missions for Okinawa Jima Invasion Forces, 24-26 Apr., 1945.
Support Missions for Okinawa Jima Invasion Forces, 28-30 Apr., 1945.
Support Missions for Okinawa Jima Invasion Forces, 2-5 May, 1945.
Support Missions for Okinawa Jima Invasion Forces, 7-13 May, 1945.
Support Missions for Okinawa Jima Invasion Forces, 11-13 May, 1945.
Support Missions for Okinawa Jima Invasions Forces, 11-13 May, 1945.
Raid on Kyushu for Okinawa Jima Invasion Forces, 13-14 May, 1945.
Support Missions for Okinawa Jima Invasion Forces, 17-18 May, 1945.
Support Missions for Okinawa Jima Invasion Forces, 20 May, 1945.
Support Missions for Okinawa Jima Invasion Forces, 20-26 May, 1945.
Support Missions for Okinawa Jima Invasion forces, 28 May, 1945.
Raid on Tokyo for Okinawa Jima Invasion Forces, 10 July, 1945.
Raid on Hokkaido and Northern Honshu, 14-15 July, 1945.
Raid on Tokyo, 18 July 1945.
Raid on Kure Naval Base, 24-25 July 1945.
Raid on Kure Naval Base, 28 July, 1945.
Raid on Tokyo, 30 Aug. 1945.
Raid on Hokkaido and Northern Honshu, 9-10 Aug. 1945.
Raid on Tokyo, 13 Aug., 2945.
Raid on Tokyo, 13 Aug., 1945.
Raid on Tokyo, 15 Aug. 1945.

I continued serving aboard the Essex until after the surrender of the Japanese and until the ship was secured in Bremerton, Washington. For this service I was granted the right to wear the American Theatre of War Ribbon, the Asiatic-Pacific Ribbon with five stars, a Philippines Liberation Medal, a Victory Medal, and a Presidential Unit Citation.

Many others who were aboard at the time the war ended served longer than I had served. Some of the crew members boarded the ship when it was commissioned in December, 1942. Their merit awards were greater than mine, and they deserved them.

There were too many happenings during this action-packed tour of duty to include in this letter. You probably would not be interested in reading about them anyway. There are, however, some experiences that I encountered that you might appreciate.

There were not a lot of recreational activities aboard ship. The restricted environment under the given circumstances didn't allow them. There were, of course, certain activities that were available to everyone. One source of such entertainment was the evening movie.

Many of the shipmates would moan when the title of some old movie was announced as the night's entertainment. I was not among the moaners. Not having been allowed to go to the movies during my youth, every movie, regardless of how ancient it was, was a night's entertainment for me.

One evening there was an experience for all who attended the show. As the movie was being shown on the metal hangar deck, to a large audience, a loud hissing sound broke loose. To almost everyone there this meant the beginning of a torpedo explosion. We knew we were hit. It was immediately mass hysteria. Everyone ran for the ladders leading to the upper deck. The ladders could not begin to handle the traffic. The enlisted men and officers alike started climbing over one another's bodies in order to get to the top of the ladder in an attempt to get topside before the explosion. When some half of the men had successfully made their exit and all the benches were strewn about the deck, it was realized that a fire extinguisher had sprung a leak. This ordeal frightened me. I wasn't accustomed to having a herd of animals use my head for a rung of a ladder.

In addition to the movies, I enjoyed talking to the catapult crew. When my work was over I would go to my stateroom, wash up, and return to the catapult section. There was never any shortage of conversation with the crew. They were a fine group of men. (About 20 years after the war I informed Norman Meinert, an elevator operator near the catapult, that I was traveling through his city in Wisconsin with my family. He suggested that we meet at a nearby restaurant. When we arrived at the restaurant we were greeted with exceptional hospitality. Norman had his whole family there, including his parents, and he had a separate room set aside for the occasion. It was a tremendous welcome. You children were all very young at this time but you will probably remember how we were truly honored.)

The catapult area was also a place of refuge. On occasions I would ignore my superior semi-private quarters below and sleep on a bunk in the catapult section, where a nighttime torpedo would be less likely to kill me. It was also a much safer area than the flight deck during battle. It was a place where I could retreat to from the flight deck and get some quick cover while the ship would be under attack. I still have a good feeling for the catapult section and its crew.

There was one incident while working with a catapult crew which resulted in a real tragedy. When a plane would be placed on the catapult by the crew, it would always be headed toward the bow of the ship. The fore part of the plane by means of its propeller would, of course, generate thrust for takeoff. A hold cable would therefore be attached to the rear of the plane to counteract this thrust. It was important for a pilot whose plane was being positioned on the catapult to avoid stepping on the brakes while the cables were being tightened. Pressure on the brakes would tend to flatten the tires and resist the required tightening of the tension cable. If after the cable was tightened, the pilot would release his unintended but existing pressure on the brake, the tires would expand upward, which in turn would cause the catch-cable at the rear of the plane to come unhooked. If such a disconnection would not be observed by the pilot his plane would drift forward.

That's exactly what happened during one of my launches where I was the dispatcher. The pilot unintentionally placed pressure on the brakes of his plane while he was being positioned on the catapult. During this time he kept looking downward inside the cockpit, evidently checking his gear. While doing this he took his feet off the brakes, releasing the pressure on the tires. This caused a release of the tail hook. The plane commenced drifting forward. I repeatedly yelled at the pilot. I pounded on the wings of his plane, but he was preoccupied with attending to something within the cockpit. The plane drifted over the bow, and the ship ran over him. He was killed. I still think about that tragedy from time to time. If I had only had something in my hand that I could have thrown at the plane's hatch, perhaps the pilot could have been saved. I'm sure the crew members would like to have done the same.

The catapult area was not always a safe area. On one occasion a kamikaze was diving down at the Essex from the starboard side. Thinking it was headed for the bridge, I jumped onto the catwalk near the catapult room, ready to dive inside in the event of a hit. Suddenly I realized that the kamikaze pilot was headed directly for the catapult section. I whirled around, climbed over the catwalk cables, and prepared for a jump into the ocean. As I was in the initial stage of a springing motion to jump, the ship's five-inch gunners hit the kamikaze and flipped the plane over the ship. When it was over, my feet had not yet left their footing, and I was clinging to the cables on the catwalk of the ship with only the tips of my fingers. I was shaky, but I retained enough strength to pull myself back into the catwalk and into the catapult room.

Judging the intended point of impact of a kamikaze was not easy. The kamikaze pilots were not as proficient as were the Japanese fighter or bomber pilots. But they were capable of hitting their target. One thing we could generally rely on, the kamikaze, if he would survive the gun fire, would either hit his target or overshoot it. This was probably due to the fact that never before in his flying career did he fly at such a fast speed.

One day during intense fighting, I had just finished dispatching the planes when I observed a kamikaze diving at us from the port side toward the stern. I intently watched and scrutinized his line of flight. I decided he was going to strike the middle of the flight deck or starboard bow. I therefore ran toward the stern of the ship and jumped into the port-side catwalk. Just as I entered the catwalk, the plane suddenly pulled out of his dive and crossed over our ship. I knew then that he had dropped a bomb and that I was right in line of the drop. I was about to be blasted. With my flash-proof gear in place, I squatted down and made myself about as small as a basketball. I felt like I was about the size of a mouse. A moment later, there it was, a tremendous explosion right beneath me under the ship. The explosion lifted the entire rear quarter of this huge forty-five-thousand-ton carrier right out of the water. I hung on to the metal of the catwalk with all my might.

When the ship became stabilized, I went forward to the bow of the flight deck to observe the only plane that was not dispatched, an F6F. Its fuselage was cracked. When the rear end of the carrier dropped back into the water it snapped its bow upward with such force that it broke the fuselage of this tubby, rugged plane. The only effect the explosion had on the ship itself was that of a free cleanup job. It knocked all the debris off the bottom of the hull. It left a slight indentation in the hull, but it did no major harm. In fact, it gave the ship three more knots of speed. Everyone was hoping that the damage would be just enough to force us back to the States for repair. No such luck!

The Essex was not to complete its duty unscathed. On the 25th day of November, 1944, general quarters was called. All hands (all personnel) rushed to their battle stations. I was in the catapult room. The planes had previously been launched. All of a sudden there was an explosion. The Essex was hit. A kamikaze dived into the Essex from the starboard side, supposedly intending to hit the middle of the flight deck. He missed his mark, but he did hit the port side of the deck, exploding a warhead in the gunnery section. It killed and injured several men and did extensive damage to the ship. Because of this hit the Essex was out of commission temporarily.

The firemen and the cleanup crews immediately responded to the disaster, as did every other available person who was able to lend a hand. Before too long things were under control. The cleanup crews took over. (I have a few feet of movies of the aftermath of this hit on the Essex.)

Everyone aboard at that time was convinced that after being so badly damaged our chances of going back to the States were great. Not so. With the parts made available to us from another ship, the Essex was repaired at sea. There was no turning back toward the U.S. Every bit of power the fleet had to offer would be utilized against the enemy.

Typhoons on the ocean created a do-or-die challenge to all hands aboard. In December of 1944 the fleet set a course westward in an attempt to escape an approaching storm. But we got caught and were forced to ride it out during the night. The waves reached a height of seventy-five feet.

During the storm a destroyer escort declared an emergency and attempted to come alongside the Essex in order to take on some fuel. It needed the fuel in order for the crew to keep the ship under control. Everyone available tried to give some assistance. It was to no avail. The destroyer escort was forced to cast off. That night, the escort, and one other, capsized. Both ships and their respective crews were lost. On the following day the log book of the Essex stated:

> Launched an afternoon search for straggling ships and survivors of ships that floundered during typhoon.

The search continued unsuccessfully for three days. Similar notations were made in the ship's log. On the fourth day the search was abandoned.

Besides the loss of the two ships, other ships were seriously damaged. A couple of other major vessels had their bows twisted off; steel bows were crushed as if they were made of tin.

Eating during these storms was itself a battle. All the benches and chairs would be tied down. No food could be placed on the table. The members of the crew would take only what they could hold in their hands. It was practically impossible to walk without holding on to something solid. It was even difficult to get to where the emergency rations were being handed out.

On January 9, 1945, after dark, the fleet set a course for the Bashi Channel to enter the China Sea. The purpose of this action was to search the area for the Japanese fleet and to support our invasion forces on northern Luzon. On January 16, the log of the Essex stated that we were 125 miles from Hong Kong. During the latter part of January the fleet steamed en route to and through the Balintang Channel, north of Luzon, to pass from the China Sea to the Pacific Ocean.

The battle that took place when we made our exit from the China Sea was the most frightening of them all. It was a night battle. We knew we were going to be attacked with everything the Japanese had in the area. The Japanese, of course, knew the location of our fleet. They also knew that if our fleet would attempt to pass through any of the straits in that area they could reach us with their land-based planes.

Everyone was tense as we approached the straits. All hands were at their battle stations waiting for the enemy. Suddenly there they came, from all directions, dropping flares, torpedoes, and bombs. They also strafed our ship with their low-level-attack planes. (I don't remember whether or not kamikazes were used in the attack.) All our ships were firing. Much of our firepower was aimed at the low-flying enemy aircraft. This caused our firepower to cross the decks of our own ships.

Our carriers fired only their 40mm guns. This was to deceive the Japanese pilots. If the Japanese pilots were to see 5-inch guns firing they would know that such action could very well be from an aircraft carrier. They would thereupon aim for the ship firing the larger guns.

Kamikaze hit on the U.S.S. Essex 11/25/1944.

The night battle ignited the sky. Several hundred New York forth of July celebrations could not have created more noise or surprise. This was due to the hundreds of parachute flares dropped by the Japanese and the millions of tracer (red-burning) bullets that were being fired by the Japanese and by our fleet. (Every fifth bullet was a tracer. The gunners, by watching the tracers, could see where they were actually shooting.) During this battle I felt as though a total destruction of our fleet was a definite possibility.

For some reason, which I don't remember, I was on the port side of the bow, down in the catwalk. I wanted to get across the deck so I could get into the catapult room. It was mightily scary down in that catwalk all alone during this nighttime battle. Notwithstanding all the firing that was taking place, I decided to make a run across the deck and try for a safer spot, the catapult room. But I couldn't move. My legs were limp. They wouldn't work. And it was lucky I couldn't move. Bullets started whizzing right over the flight deck where I would have gone. When the bullets started going directly over my head, I decided to stay right were I was. I remained in my exceedingly vulnerable position until the shooting stopped.

I don't remember how long that battle lasted. But it seemed like a lifetime.

After having served months aboard the U.S.S. Bougainville and several months aboard the Essex, I was getting mighty tired of ocean duty. We would occasionally hear rumors about the Essex being ordered back to the States for an overhaul. This would lift the spirits of the men for a few days. But when it would be learned that the rumors were false, the same old gloom would reappear on the faces of the crew. Then one day there was good news.

During a Sunday-morning worship service, when we were about two-thirds through, the overhead speaker clicked on. This was usual during a religious service. Everyone was tense. Then the Captain's voice: "This is the Captain speaking." I don't remember his exact words, but the gist of his statement was that the Essex was being temporarily relieved for repair somewhere in the States.

The Chaplin, with a cracking sound in his voice, said, "That's all for today; our prayers have been answered." Everyone yelled with joy. The tune "California Here We Come" was immediately played over the communication system after the Captain's announcement. I headed for the catapult room. Some of the men along my route were screaming, some were dancing, some were crying, and some looked stunned and displayed a somber, motionless look. This was a deep emotional time for everyone aboard. Just a couple of more engagements with the Japanese and we would be on our way.

The next few engagements, however, were disastrous. I believe they took place during the Okinawa invasion. Six of our eleven major carriers were hit. Our orders to return to the States were canceled. We would remain with the fleet until the end of the war.

After several engagements and a long time out at sea, the Essex pulled in bay at the Ulithi Islands, where it was replenished around the clock. While here the crew members got alternate four-day passes to go ashore.

The air group also exchanged some of their old or damaged planes for new ones during this period of time. The old or damaged planes that could fly were flown from the ship to a landing strip on the island. From there they were flown to Guam. At Guam new planes would be exchanged for the old ones. The new ones would then be flown back to Ulithi. I was assigned to fly one of the old planes to Guam. While I had had a considerable amount of flying time and a lot of experience dispatching planes by means of the catapult, I had not had the personal experience of being catapulted. Experience or not, all the old planes on deck were to be catapulted off. I was assigned to fly one of them. Normally this would not be so bad, but on this occasion the planes were to be catapulted from the ship while the ship was anchored, and with very little wind. I was the first to go. I had the feeling the Commander was using me as a guinea pig.

After making sure I had everything in good order, I gave the readiness signal to the dispatcher. He in turn gave the order to the catapult crew, they released the pressure, and off I went. I made sure to lift the wheels on my plane as soon as I left the deck. I wanted to dress the plane as quickly as possible so it would have minimum drag and have the benefit of a flat belly on the plane for a water landing in the event I would not be able to gain sufficient flying speed. I also wanted the catapult crew to know that I was a competent pilot. All went well. I was soon airborne. After circling the area, I landed on a nearby air strip. Here my plane like the rest of our planes, was fueled in preparation for our fight to Guam.

The Commander took off first from the island airstrip; the rest of the squadron, including a few substitutes such as myself, followed. All seemed to be going well until my plane suddenly started to spit and sputter. I checked everything in the cockpit that could conceivably be wrong. Everything was in good order, but I was still losing altitude. I could follow the group, but I was not sure the old rattletrap that I was flying was going to make it. Happening to see a ship a fair distance away and deciding I probably would not make it to Guam, I peeled away from the squadron for a crash landing near the sighted ship. When I got closer to the ship, I recognized it as something other than an American vessel. I was now between the devil and the deep blue sea. I could still see the air group at a distance; so I chose to follow the squadron toward an area that I knew would be safe, if I could make it. I was apprehensive about my chances for survival at this juncture of the flight, but the island of Guam finally came into sight. What a blessing!

The landing strip on the island was, of course, above sea level. The trick now was to get the plane high enough to keep from hitting the ground before landing. I informed the airport tower of my plight. The air controller gave me emergency landing clearance, and the old plane was good to me. With the help of a few updrafts over the ground area I was able to make a safe and uneventful landing.

I don't recall the exact month I landed on Guam. I believe it was in the spring of 1945. While there, I went down to the submarine base and made inquiry about the submarine Sea Wolf. My friend from Calvin College, John VanAndel, was aboard that submarine. When I asked whether the Sea Wolf

On Ulithi Island with former student (left) and former cadet friend (right).

would by chance happen to be in port, the seaman at the counter asked me to stand by. He went into the back room. An officer came out with the seaman and asked why I was seeking information about the Sea Wolf. I told him about my friend being aboard, and that if the submarine would happen to be in port I would like to get in touch with him. They then informed me that the Sea Wolf was not in port and that they could give me no information about its location. I later learned that the Sea Wolf had been sunk during the previous October somewhere near Japan, and that my good friend, along with the entire crew, had been lost.

I returned to the Ulithi Islands with a new F6F plane. While there, I flew a couple of patrol flights and then went back aboard the Essex, for whatever the future had to offer.

Aboard the ship were a few men from Grand Rapids, Michigan. One of them was a pilot who was attached to Air Group 83. This pilot took part in several major assaults against enemy targets. Generally, pre-dawn flights were scheduled for these attacks. During my dispatching of the torpedo planes on one of these scheduled assignments, the pilot from Grand Rapids taxied up next to me and into position for takeoff. I signaled him to rev up the engine. This he did. I was dubious about the efficiency of his plane's engine. It didn't sound right. I then signaled for him to add more power. He tried. I suspected that one of the magnetos was malfunctioning; so I gave a thumb-down signal. The commanding officer on the bridge ordered me to send him off, but I refused. This plane was loaded with explosives. The poor performance of the engine would most probably have meant an immediate crash into the sea. The air officer gave a second order for me through my "talker" who was the direct medium to me from the bridge. I declined the order and motioned the pilot over to the side of the deck, next to the bridge. I then launched the remaining planes.

I knew I was in trouble for refusing to obey the commanders' orders. But I knew I was right and that I had probably saved a life and an expensive airplane.

Immediately following the launch the downed plane was lowered to the hangar deck for immediate examination, and the pilot was ordered to stay in the cockpit. In very short order the air commander and the V-2 (aircraft maintenance division officer were in conference next to the plane. I was correct in my judgment assessment of the problem. No action was taken against me.

One bright and sunny day the fleet was warned that a Japanese attack was on its way. An immediate dispatch of the planes was ordered by the Captain. I successfully launched every plane except one located at the rear of the flight deck. I motioned to him to taxi into position, but he wouldn't move. I repeated my signal. He still would not move. I started over to his plane to find out if there was a problem. At that moment a plane buzzed over me, about twenty feet above my head. I looked up. There was a large Japanese rising sun insignia on the bottom of a wing. Before I could do anything, the plane passed over the flight deck. It crashed into the side of a nearby ship. The pilot on board of our ship was obviously waiting to see what the Japanese plane was going to do before taxiing into its line of flight.

No special duties were assigned to me during landing operations. I would often sit in a room adjacent to the flight deck and directly under the bridge while the planes were landing. There would generally be some maintenance personnel there, and occasionally some officers from the bridge would come down and join the coffee kletz. On a few occasions I had the privilege of talking to Admiral Byrd, who was a visiting admiral, during our coffee break.

Firemen, maintenance men, and flight deck crewmen were always present during the landings. It was no rare occasion for a combination of these men to rescue a pilot or a crewman from a plane crash, a burning plane, or a plane that had been riddled with bullets. When called upon to do so, they would also tenderly remove the wounded and the dead. The wounded were rushed to the ship's hospital. The dead would be given a burial at sea. In some instances the dead pilot or crew member would be dumped into the sea along with the bullet riddled plane, a solemn event. The deep feeling of those attending the burial could only be expressed with absolute silence as the plane descended beneath the surface of the sea.

The Essex was never in the Battle of Midway; that battle was before its time. But the movie "The Battle of Midway" showed some crashes and a burial of a pilot with his plane that took place aboard the Essex. I recognized the crashes and burial when I saw the movie. I had jumped out of the way of some of the crashes that were shown in the picture. (Some of the accidents in the movie involved F6F's. During The Battle of Midway there were no F6F's. They were F4F's, a smaller plane.)

Some of the most admired men aboard the Essex were the gunners, especially those who manned the five-inch guns. A few of them were from the hill country. They must have been squirrel hunters since they were old enough to walk. Besides knowing it was do or die against the kamikazes, they were determined to make a hit. They repeatedly saved the Essex from getting blown out of the ocean.

An example of the talent and skill of these men was evidenced during an extensive air-to-ship engagement during which a Japanese bomber was approaching another aircraft carrier from its stern. The crew members on that carrier were evidently unaware of this approaching enemy plane. Its gunners were probably concentrating on danger ahead. Without hesitation and with complete accuracy the men in the five-inchers on the Essex turned their guns toward our sister carrier and with one shot blew the Japanese plane to bits when it was within a few hundred feet from its target.

While the U.S. Navy was first class and was the most powerful navy in the world, many of our ships, especially our aircraft carriers took a beating. I was there when some of our finest carriers were completely demolished. I remember the devastation that was inflicted upon the U.S.S. Franklin (it just kept on exploding), the U.S.S. Enterprise, the Bunker Hill, and the U.S.S. Ticonderoga (it took two kamikazes right on the flight deck within minutes of each other.) There were others too, but I cannot remember all of them at this stage of my life.

I was especially sensitive about the Ticonderoga assault. As I stated before, its Captain, Dixie Kiefer, had been my commanding officer at Olathe, Kansas. He had also been the Executive Officer on the Yorktown when it was sunk during The Battle of Midway. When the new Yorktown was being constructed, he was expected to be its commander. But when it was ready to be launched and commissioned, Captain Kiefer's leg was still not healed from the injuries he suffered during The Battle of Midway. He was therefore assigned to one of the next available carriers, which turned out to be the new Ticonderoga.

When the Ticonderoga was hit, it was the only ship that was attacked. It was peculiar the way it happened. The Essex which was the desired and preferred target of the Japanese, because of its successful record and reputation, pulled out of the center of the fleet to launch its fighter planes. From the air it would appear to be the least protected carrier at the time, a great target for the kamikazes. Yet they chose the Ticonderoga, which was surrounded with destroyers and battleships.

It was the opinion of several aboard the Essex that the kamikazes probably thought that the ship in the center of the fleet, which looked like the Essex (it was of the Essex class), was in fact the Essex they wanted to be the ones to get the prize. This would not only please the Emperor but would give "Tokyo Rose" (a Japanese newscaster) the news she had been waiting for — the destruction of the Essex. On a previous occasion she had mistakenly reported that the Essex had been sunk. Whatever the reason for the kamikazes choosing the Ticonderoga, the destruction to this great ship was a tragedy. It was a new and beautiful ship, but it unfortunately had a relatively inexperienced crew of fine young men. (Captain Kiefer was not injured during this attack. He, however, was killed after the war when his plane crashed into a mountain in upper New York.)

Between battles there was ample time to relax. On many occasions I would go to the forecastle, an open section of the bow under the flight deck. It was there that I would reminisce. This huge war-ship cruising over the boundless ocean caused me on many occasions to reflect on my own significance. When I would concentrate on the fact that there were over three thousand sailors aboard our ship; that the Essex was only one of the thousands of ships upon the ocean; that all navies of the world only comprise a small percentage of the total military personnel; that all the armies and navies of the world constituted only a fraction of the world population, I realized that one little person such as myself didn't amount to much.

Diminution of my importance, however, did not deter me from reflecting on my youth, the possibility of survival, my relationship to my Creator, my religious customs, old girlfriends, future ambitions, etc. It was here, too, that I would sometimes take my mail and read it.

When I first arrived on the Essex I received a considerable amount of mail. I received a few letters from my Mexican-American acquaintance. She indicated that she was intrigued by my Dutch customs and that she would like to give them a try. I also, initially, enjoyed regular correspondence with the navy nurse in Honolulu. After several months at sea this exchange of letters with the nurse terminated. I didn't know for sure whether she stopped writing, whether she was transferred to a location where sending mail would be difficult, or whether some of the mail was not getting through. I also enjoyed letters from friends and family.

Mealtime aboard ship, like mail time, was generally enjoyable. During scheduled battle days the entire crew would be given steak for breakfast. This was not my favorite time to eat steak, but when I would realize that there might not be any food available during what could be a long and arduous battle it wasn't too hard to accept.

On noncombat days we would be fed cafeteria style. One noon hour as I was going through the line, getting some food on a plate, one of the black cooks reeled out some obnoxious and threatening remarks at me with a peculiar look in his eyes. He couldn't have been mad at me. I didn't know him and he didn't know me. I never made any complaints about the food; the food aboard the ship was in fact very good. I concluded that this man might be going off his rocker. (Becoming mentally unbalanced was a frequent occurrence aboard our ship during the latter part of the war. Some of the men had been on the ship since it was commissioned.)

Because of my concern for the safety of others, I thought I should report the incident to the Executive Officer. He could then decide whether or not to have this man examined by the medical officer. I first informed the Executive Officer's aide about the matter. Later that day the Executive Officer called me into his quarters to get more details on the happening. The Executive Officer did not seem too concerned. He discounted the need for any medical examination. After a few minutes of small talk the Executive Officer, who was a Southerner, said, "Maybe someday you Yankees will realize why we had the whipping post in the South." I was shocked. I had never come in contact with this kind of demagoguery. With a salute I took my leave. I was disenchanted with the "Exec." I had accomplished nothing. I had merely reported the abnormal conduct of one nut to another nut.

Ultimately the fighting in the Pacific started to wind down. The U.S. Navy seemed to gain control of its own destiny. But by this time all personnel aboard our ship was tired of war.

When the first atomic bomb was dropped, everyone in the fleet was made aware of it. We all knew, after the dropping of the bomb, that the war would soon be over. Following the dropping of the second "A" bomb, the war was in fact concluded. Our last scheduled raid on Tokyo was August 15, 1945. On that day our air group, CVG 83, after taking off for an attack in Tokyo, was ordered to jettison their bombs in the ocean and return to the ship. President Truman announced that the Japanese had surrendered.

The entire crew aboard the Essex was then absolutely sure that our ship Essex would be relieved of its Pacific duty — but not yet. The Essex had to remain in the area until after the signing of the peace treaty, and until after the occupation of Japan was given some initial support.

On August 20 the U.S.S. Wasp replaced the Essex. The Essex was ordered to join task group 38.4, which consisted of the U.S.S. Missouri (on which the peace treaty was to be signed) and several other great ships. Our ship's log from August 20th through the August 31st, 1945, is as follows:

20 Replenishing as before. During the afternoon watch the WASP joined TG 38.3 and took the station regularly assigned ESSEX. Pursuant to ComThirdFleet orders Essex was detached from TG 38.3 and joined 38.4 which comprised the MISSOURI with Adm. W.F. Halsey ComThird Fleet embarked, SHANGRI-LA with Vice Adm. J.S. McCain CTF 38 and ComSecTask For embarked, YORKTOWN with Rear Adm. A.W. Radford CTG 38.4 and ComCarDive 6 embarked, HMS DUKE OF YORK withVice Adm. Rawlings, RN, CTF 38 embarked; the BON HOMME RICHARD, COWPENS, INDEPENDENCE, WISCONSIN, FLINT, QUINCY, BOSTON, CHICAGO, ST. PAUL, ATLANTA, DAYTON, HMS NEWFOUNDLAND, HMS GAMBIA, 18 U.S. destroyers and 3 British destroyers. A typhoon was located 300 miles SE of the disposition. 30-58N; 144-06 BE.

21 Refueling and replenishing as before, the typhoon has moved to a position 180 miles NNE of the disposition and an inter-tropical front lies over the disposition of a NE-SW line. 31-06N; 143-09E.

22 Steaming in same general area in TG 38.4 transferring F6F spare parts to MERRIMAC for further transfer to the SHANGRI-LA. The typhoon had passed well clear to a position 550 miles north of the disposition. 31-36N; 142-34E.

23 Third Fleet reorganized and reformed in accordance with ComThird Fleet Op. Orders 10-45, 11-45, and 12-45 to conduct Operations in support of the occupation of Japan. The following units were detached from TG 38.4 HMS DUKE OF YORK, KING GEORGE V, NEW FOUNDLAND, GAMBIA, WELT, NIZAN, NAPIER, the U.S.S. MISSOURI, COWPENS, QUINCY, BOSTON, ST. PAUL, and 11 destroyers joined TG

38.4 The Task Groups of TF 38 proceeded to operate independently, TG 38.4 to an area about 120 miles SE of Najimo Saki of SE Honsh u. 33-33N; 144-O8E.

24-28 Steaming in TG 38.4 in an area 100-150 miles SE of the SE tip of Honshu conducting air operations in support of the occupation of Japan. Operations included Airfield Reconnaissance Missions, Prisoner of War Camp Searches, Targe CAPs over Atsugi, Tokyo Bay, and Sagami Bay, an TG CAPs.

24 35-15N; 144-02E.

25 34-57N; 142-08E.

26 34-33N; 142-09E.

27 34-27N; 141-59E.

28 34-24N; 141-56E.

29-30 Refueling and reprovisioning in area bounded by 32N, 30N, 142E, and 144E. Also transferred replacement planes to other carriers of TG 38.4. Commenced receiving personnel from ships of TG 38.4 for transportation to the U.S.

29 31-53N; 142-53E.

30 31-45N; 142-48E.

31 Operating in TG 38.4 in area about 100 miles SE of Tokyo Bay conducting air operations in support of the occupation of Japan. Launched Airfield Reconnaissance Missions, Target CAPS over Atsugi, Tokyo Bay and Sagami Bay, patrols, searches and TG CAPS. Continued receiving personnel for transportation to the United States. 34-32N; 142-17E.

During this interim period of time, between the cease-fire and the signing of the peace treaty, I was able to get my required flight time by taking flights as a passenger in a torpedo bomber. One of the flights was over Tokyo.

Our flight over Tokyo was at a very low altitude. The remains of the city revealed the unbelievable assaults that it had experienced. The main building structures within the city were flattened. People who happened to be walking on the streets when we flew over would turn their back toward our plane. However, the prisoner of war camp was intact, as was Hirohito's palace. Also, some electric trains were providing limited transportation.

The news finally reached us that the formal unconditional surrender would be signed by the Japanese aboard the U.S.S. Missouri (which represented President Truman's home state) on the 2nd day of September, 1945, in Tokyo Harbor.

Before the actual signing of the surrender a show of U.S. air and sea power was masterfully displayed. Included in this show of forces were countless ships, and airplanes of all types as far as the eye could see. I presume this display of power was for the purpose of showing the Japanese the tremendous amount of reserve that was available to the United States in the event they would ever consider reneging on their agreement to sign the proposed unconditional surrender, or ever consider attacking the United States at a future date.

After the surrender was signed and sufficient support was given for the initial steps toward the occupation of Japan, the Essex was refueled and loaded with cargo and men. On September 3rd the Essex was ordered to steam to Puget Sound, Washington. I can't recall any cheering aboard the ship when the word came that the surrender had been formally signed, but I do remember repeated cheers when we were given the word that we were definitely on our way back to the States.

Our homeward route brought us northward near Anchorage, Alaska, where the weather became inclement and cold. The days en route were anxious ones. Each day seemed like a week.

As the ship steamed toward the state of Washington, everyone began talking about seeing a lighted city again. We had been in blackout conditions during the entire war. On our ship if anyone would open one of the ship's exit hatches at night to go out onto a catwalk, or out onto the forecastle, the person making the exit would be in complete darkness. No light could be seen anywhere outside of the ship, not even on our sister ships; so the thoughts of seeing a lighted city were moments of great anticipation for everyone on board.

While I was below deck, an announcement came over the intercom system that the city of Seattle had been sighted. Everyone not on duty went topside. The ship's log on September 13, 1945, states:

> Steaming as before. 0450 Changed course to 120+T. 0453Passed SLIP POINT light beam to starboard, distance 5 miles. 0500 Ran into fog bank, visibility decreased to about 1,000 yards. 0529Changed course to 100+T. 0545 Changed course to 909+T. 0558 Changed course to 095+T. 0559 Changed speed to 5 knots.0604 Changed course to 075+T. 0612 Changed course to 9050+T. 0617 Changed course to 100+T. 0622 Stopped all engines. 0625 Commenced sounding fog signals. 0634 Changed speed to 5knots. 0635 Changed course to 270+T. 0646 Changed course to 090+T. 0617 Changed course to 100+T. 0622 Stopped allengines. 062 Commenced sounding fog signals. 0634 Changed speed to 5 knots. 0635 Changed course to 270+T. 0646 Changed course to 090+T. 0649 Changed speed to 10 knots. 0721 Changed course to 110+T. 0759 Changed speed to 5 knots, changed course to 080+T. Average R.P.M. 104.6.

Many of the men stayed on the flight deck during the entire night, just to look at the lights of the city. Some men on board had not seen a lighted city for over three years.

The Essex was held in the harbor until September 15th, a Saturday. During the morning hours the ship began to steam toward a berth in Puget Sound.

> Anchored as before. 0800 Mustered crew on stations; no absentees. 0807 Lighted fires under boilers Nos. 1, 3, 5 and 8. 0910 Cut in boilers Nos. 1, 3, 5 and 8 in on the main steamline. 9030 Pursu-

ant to Commanding Officer's order No. 771 dated 15 September 1945, Lieutenant Commander G. DONNELLEY, (A) USNR (128508) was detached this date to report to Commandant THIRTEENTH Naval District for temporary duty pending discharge. 1100 Made all preparations for getting underway. 1130 Got underway for PUGET SOUND NAVY YARD, Captain at conn, Executive Officer and Navigator on the bridge, standard speed 15 knots, standing out of berth No. 21 off INDIAN ISLAND, PUGET SOUND on various courses conforming to the channel. Average R.P.M. 133.0.

Before docking, all the officers and men were given specific duties that would be assigned to them while in port. I had several assignments as Officer of the Deck. I also was designated as one of the officers who would be participating in a victory parade. Being assigned duties as Officer of the Deck, I could understand, but having to take part in a parade was, to me, an exercise in futility.

Prior to having to practice drill procedures, I, like everyone aboard, was given alternate passes to go into the city. Before I left the ship I was given a message to call a certain number. I telephoned the number. It was my old roommate from Olathe, Kansas, Gene Geary, who knew I was aboard the Essex. He was getting married and wanted me to walk his bride-to-be down the aisle during the ceremony. Her parents lived in Pontiac, Michigan, and they were unable to travel to Seattle for the wedding. I rushed right over to his apartment for an old-time get together. While there, I was given instructions regarding the arrangements. It was a small wedding, due to the fact that all of the bride's and groom's relatives were in the Midwest, but it was a very meaningful ceremony.

One of my own personal priorities was to see if I could locate the navy nurse whom I had not heard from for several months. I realized it would be a long shot for her to be transferred from Hawaii to Seattle, but I thought I could give it a try. I called the naval station in Seattle, where some of the nurses were housed. I asked if by chance my friend would be registered there. The person who answered my call said she had no one listed on the roster at the station by the name I had given her, but that there was some new transferees who had just checked in. She then called a nurse to the phone who had just arrived from Hawaii along with several others. As a special assist I informed this new arrival of my friend's nickname. With this information she asked me to wait a moment. After a few minutes of waiting, my friend came to the phone. I identified myself and got a very pleasant but reserved reaction. She stated in a meaningful way that she was indeed glad that I had survived the war. After a few verbal pleasantries back and forth, she informed me that the reason they had a difficult time locating her at the barracks was because her name had been changed. She had married. I wasn't prepared for this. Not having dated for about a year and having anticipated picking this relationship up where it left off in Honolulu, I was, needless to say, stunned. It was a dramatic experience for me to be confronted with such an irreversible reality. After informing me of her marriage, she reluctantly told me that her husband had been killed in the war.

With the right to a week's leave, I decided to take a bus to Astoria, Oregon, for the purpose of picking up my car. I called my friends in Astoria and asked them if they would call the garage owner and have him get my car ready to travel. They were rather excited about my having survived the war and that I would be stopping at their house to pay them a visit.

When the bus arrived at the station in Astoria, much to my surprise, two of my friends were there to greet me, the mother and one of her daughters. I never expected anyone to be at the station. I had intended to pick up my car and then drive to their home. But my automobile wasn't ready; so they graciously came to give me an assist.

The garage owner was unable to get my car ready in such short order. He said it needed a couple of parts and a tune-up, but he promised it for the following day. I was invited to stay overnight at the home of my friends, and, if I remember correctly, I accepted this invitation.

The following day I recalled having left my electric shaver at the drug store for repair before I set out to sea. I still had the claim check in my wallet. I presented it to the store owner. He smiled and said that all such things left over ninety (90) days were sold. My shaver was gone. But the druggist was fair, he gave me another one similar to the one I had left with him.

With my car fixed and a substitute shaver retrieved, I thanked my friends for their kindness and hospitality and left the quaint city of Astoria for a return to the Essex.

Upon reaching Seattle from Astoria, with my car now available for transportation, I decided to give my old girlfriend another call. With some reluctance on both sides we decided to go out to dinner. During our time together it was self-evident that she was deeply grieved over her husband's death. She stated that she had married an army pilot who was sent to Guam and that while there, and while he was sleeping, some Japanese guerrillas slipped inside his tent and slit his throat. We saw each other a few more times. However, time and circumstances made it self-evident that a renewal of a courtship was not probable.

Parade time was approaching. With a case of moderate battle fatigue and the other depressive news that I encountered, I did not feel like marching in a parade. I would have given anything to get out of it. No such luck. Furthermore, I had to be one of the first half dozen leading the Essex crew.

During the celebration, other units participated in the march. I could hear the crowd clapping for the other groups as we approached the grandstand. When the Essex section came into view of the spectators they screamed and whistled. I wasn't ready for such forceful action by onlookers. It intimidated me. A large number of navy WAVES were also there cheering and yelling. I learned afterward that the Essex had been given a great deal of publicity during the war. It was probably because of this that it was an honor for the community to have the Essex in its local port and to be able to give the gallant men of this great ship a personal thanks.

When we reached the end of the parade route, several of the WAVES were there to join in the festivities. One of the WAVES appeared to me to be quite attractive, and she kept smiling at me. We eventually said hello to each other. She was from Saginaw, Michigan. Both being from Michigan, we had something to talk about.

My Officer of the Deck duties were routine except for one occasion. During my hours on duty on a certain day, two seamen were to deliver the Captain's jeep to a certain location. Before performing their duties they decided to get a couple of friends and buzz around the city. Little did they realize that driving a jeep around a corner on a street at a high rate of speed would bring a different result than if they were driving an automobile. As luck would have it, they turned a corner too fast, turned the jeep over, and damaged it.

When the men returned to the ship, they came directly to me as Officer of the Deck, but also as an officer who they knew would try to help them out of a mess. I told them to get the jeep over to the body shop, to tell the mechanics to fix it as quickly as possible, and to bring a temporary replacement jeep for the Captain. I didn't put the accident on the ship's log and punished no one. These young men had been out to sea for an extensive period of time. I wasn't about to do something that would cause them to be confined. It appeared as if things were working out fairly well, until I got a call from a superior officer.

My philosophical explanation of tolerance and forgiveness to these gallant young men who had made a measly little mistake with the Captain's jeep didn't fly. I was restricted to the ship for one week. My confinement, however, did not preclude my having guests come aboard. My friend Geary and his new wife and my new WAVE friend from Michigan visited me during my confinement. We all had dinner aboard ship.

Shortly after I completed my week's confinement, I was given a two-weeks' leave. When some of the seamen on board the Essex heard I was going on leave and drive my car to Michigan, they thought they would do something great for me. As I was leaving the ship, I was given a handwritten letter and told to read it later. While walking to my car, I opened the letter and read it. The letter was from the men who wrecked the jeep. It stated that they deeply appreciated the sacrifice that I had made on their behalf. The letter also stated that they had delivered four new tires for my car to a certain gas station. (They knew my car had bad tires.) They also had made arrangements for the tires to be put on my car without cost to me. I presumed the tires were extra jeep tires from the ship. Not attempting to find out, I drove home on my old tires. I did, however, appreciate their kind thoughts.

Before leaving for Michigan, I received several requests from shipmates to ride along and share expenses. I consented to take four of them. We all agreed to take turns at the wheel and to drive straight through from Seattle to Michigan. However, one of the shipmates' inability to operate a motor vehicle, plus his lack of driving experience over the past couple of years while on board ship, altered our schedule. At about the halfway point on our trip he failed to stop in time to avoid hitting the vehicle ahead of us. He wrecked the left front wheel and fender of my car. When this happened, my passengers took off by whatever means of transportation that was available to them, but I had to remain in order to get the wreck fixed. After a couple of days I was on the road again, and a couple of days later I was home.

I don't remember much about this homecoming other than several of the towns people told me they had heard a great deal of news about the Essex. Going to church was, of course, a must; twice on Sunday was expected. I attended the services and was given a warm welcome by the members. A few other servicemen were also home at the same time. It was good to see them. The sad part of my visit was learning how many of my friends and acquaintances had been killed. This news, combined with my own experiences and my uncertainty about my future, was disconcerting.

After having seen all of my family, having been given an update on all the local news, and having had my car fully repaired, I headed back for the ship. One of the sailors who started with me on my homeward trip met me in Chicago. He decided to ride back with me from there to the coast.

While going through the Dakotas I remembered having met a girl while visiting a college in Pella, Iowa, who lived on a farm in South Dakota near a small town. I decided to give her a call. She was home and seemed exceptionally pleased that I called her. She invited us over. We were running short of time, but I agreed to make a short stop. Finally finding the farm house — it was in the middle of nowhere — we drove up an exceptionally long driveway and stopped next to the house, whereupon she and her sister came running out to greet us. I got a big hug. I was a little embarrassed, just a little. I introduced her to my passenger friend. She introduced her sister to both of us. We were then invited into the house, where we met her parents.

Due to the limited amount of time remaining on our leave of absence, we decided to get back on the road. A thought came to mind. In order to extend our visit with the girls it would be a good idea, if they would want to ride with us to the next town, about forty miles away, and then return on the bus. The bus schedule was checked. It was perfect; so they rode along to the next town. When we arrived there, I purchased their bus tickets for their return trip.

They were interesting girls. The one girl was a schoolteacher at a one-room school. Her means of transportation to and from the school was a horse. It was intriguing to learn from them about their way of life in an area where the farms were huge.

The bus soon arrived. (If the bus would have beaten us to the station it was our intent to hail it down. Such an intercept would not have been unusual in this sparsely settled country.) When the girls boarded the bus, we proceeded on our way to the coast. Eventually we arrived back at the ship, where we reported aboard.

The remainder of my time aboard the ship was taken up with mundane duties and saying good-bye to shipmates as they left the ship for discharge centers. It was a period of mixed emotions. The thought of not seeing some of these men again was disheartening. But the assurance that they would be returning to their homes and to a peaceful environment outweighed the benefits of a continuing association.

Intermixed with my normal duties during my last days aboard ship were a few social events and a couple of get-togethers with the Gearys.

Finally it was all over, so far as the Essex was concerned. I received my orders to report to the Glenview Naval Air Station near Chicago, Illinois. I sold my car to someone on the coast. I had had enough driving for a while. I boxed my belongings and addressed the trunk for shipment to my home in Dutton, Michigan.

Before leaving the shipyard, I turned around and took one last look at the grand old Essex. In this short moment I summarily heard the roar of the planes' engines, the sound of the mighty guns, the boatswain's whistle, the general quarters alarm, the crashing of the kamikaze, the explosion of the bomb that raised the stern of the ship out of the sea, the roar of the ocean waves during the typhoon, and the sound of splashing water when the bodies of the dead were ceremoniously slipped into the sea. Now it appeared as if the fighting giant was about to go to sleep. In my heart and mind I gave the old warrior a salute and left the yard.

I cannot remember now how I traveled to Glenview, Illinois; I believe it was via train. When I arrived at Glenview, I was thoroughly examined by a physician. There was some thought of hospitalizing me for battle fatigue. I convinced the doctors that I could recover from battle fatigue just as easily at home as I could in a hospital. I was thereupon given my separation papers, which allowed me to be home for Christmas and which would release me from military service on January 1, 1946.

U.S.S. Essex- 1945.

Post war return to Dutton.

Dedication of the Gains Township Honor Roll for those who died in World War II.

Chapter XVIII.

Back Home In Dutton

I arrived home without an automobile. Little did I realize when I sold my car on the coast how impossible it would be to buy another car, especially a new one. The only automobile that could possibly be purchased without a trade-in was a Hudson. I didn't care much for the car, but I ordered one anyway. My name was put on a list, but I was to be among the many who would wait and wait for my order to be filled.

Living again with Ma and Pa in their very small house was a real adjustment. I was no longer a lieutenant. I had no status. I had no job. I had no idea what I could possibly do to make a living. I was 25 years of age. I had no girl friend, and all my old girlfriends were married. Church life seemed to be different. The home-town people were exceptionally nice, but they had, and understandably so, no deep insight into the reality of the combat that I had experienced. They had read about the battles, they had heard about the terrible results of certain military engagements, but they could not possibly sense what many of the servicemen had undergone. So I was back home in a community where I was in fact psychologically isolated.

I was not only a lonely person; I was a depressed individual who started having frightening nightmares. During periods of deep sleep I would catapult myself from the bed, sometimes against the wall, and sometimes landing on the floor. This continued for about six months.

I was daily confronted with having to make a decision concerning my future. Going back to college was out of the question. I was too nervous for that. I could not possibly sit through hour-long classes. No jobs were available. There were dozens of veterans for every decent job. Flying was out of the question. I had had my fill of airplanes. I decided that maybe a little time should be allowed to pass before making any serious decisions about what to do for a living. It was time that I should do some socializing. Sitting around during the winter months with all my miserable problems was not the answer to my problems.

Roller skating was something I used to do. Was I too old to go roller skating? I had to do something that was permissible within the church community. I decided to give roller skating a try, but I had no transportation. I indicated to Pa that I would like to go to the roller rink at Reeds Lake, about fifteen miles away. I wondered whether he would mind if I used his 11/2-ton cattle truck; he had no car. He was not inclined to let his truck out at night. I then suggested that there was a bus line at the edge of the city; if he would get me there, I could catch a bus. Once at the rink I could probably get someone to take me home. This he would do. I got my skates, got into the truck's manure-smelling cab, and, together with Pa, headed for the bus stop.

Arriving at the bus stop, I realized that the buses came at greater time intervals than I had expected, and it was already starting to get dark. The buses ran about every twenty minutes during the evening. I knew Pa didn't appreciate sitting there with his truck; so I got out of the cab and stood at the bus stop, hoping the bus would soon come. Pa took off for home.

I stood at this chilly bus stop wondering whether the bus would, in fact, come along this particular route during evening hours. After waiting for a few minutes in a standing position, I turned my skate case on its end and made a temporary seat for myself. Feeling like a totally useless human being, I started to fall asleep. (This moderate case of battle fatigue that followed me home would at times cause me to fall asleep, sometimes without warning.) I, however, was awake when the bus stopped to pick me up. I remember this waiting incident as a low point in my rehabilitation to civilian life.

I arrived at the roller rink about an hour after I was dropped off at the bus stop. I was pleasantly surprised when I entered the rink. I was met by some old friends, one of whom immediately offered to take me home when he heard of my plight. I accepted his offer. Notwithstanding the great number of younger people on the rink, there were several skaters my age, and older.

After the bus stop ordeal I was determined to get some sort of transportation. If I remember correctly, I picked up a temporary automobile to use until I got my new Hudson.

After doing nothing for a while, I decided I could possibly start a lumberyard in Dutton. The one that used to be there had folded during the war. In conjunction with this enterprise I would build some homes. This was at least a possibility. The more I realized there was nothing else available to me, the more I was convinced that I should give this two-pronged enterprise a try.

How to go about developing such a business was a real problem. I had no one to advise me. After taking care of some paper work, I ordered a couple of car loads of lumber and a semi-truck load of cement. I then purchased a small tract of land and hired a bulldozer to dig the first two basements. I began negotiating with a carpenter whom I intended to hire to put up the structures. Before signing any contracts I received a telegram from the lumber mill stating that it had stopped the cars of lumber en route because they were informed that I was going to use the lumber to build homes and not for the purpose of starting a lumberyard. No amount of explanation on my part could change the mind of the representatives of the mill. I was therefore forced to bulldoze the dirt back into the holes that I had dug for basements and to sell my cement to a nearby block company.

I was not a quitter. I decided to start a weekly auction sale for used farm machinery. I had the land that I had purchased for home sites. It was an excellent location to hold such a sale. I created some ads, ran them in the local newspaper, and placed signs on poles in certain sections of the township.

When sale day arrived, farmers brought in all their junk. About one-third of it sold. The next week the same thing happened. By the end of the third week I had so much junk left over on my small parcel of land that I had to terminate the business. By this time I was humiliated. I couldn't make anything work.

Although business was bad, my social life started to pick up. Some old boyfriends who were still unmarried started to call me, asking me to go with them to certain events and sometimes on double dates. My WAVE friend whom I had met after the parade in Washington called. She informed me that she was traveling through Grand Rapids to her home in Saginaw. I invited her out to our little house in Dutton to meet my parents. We went out to dinner during the evening she arrived. Upon leaving, she invited me to visit her in Saginaw, which I did at a later date. From this point on I started to make new friends.

I renewed my interest in playing softball. I had played on a team, The South Kent Boosters, who had won the area championship four consecutive years prior to the war. However, I decided to switch teams and play with the Dutton team after the war. We had some great games, and they were well attended by the public. One of our games went for seventeen innings. Our postwar Dutton team won the area championship two years in a row. I generally played third base, and I played well enough to be chosen to play on the annual all-star team.

Other things began to interest me. Several veterans decided to form a local chapter of the American Legion. There were only about ten of us who were at the organizational meeting. We all decided that the Legion was an honorable and worthwhile organization, and that because of this we should be part of it.

The American Legion Post of one of our neighboring towns had impressed all of us by assisting in the dedication of the roster of the veterans of our local area who were killed in the war. It was only a small group at this dedication, but it was a solemn event. Husbands, sons, and friends who had been with us before the war were now gone. The American Legion did its part in helping everyone remember and honor those who paid the ultimate sacrifice so that the rest of us could enjoy our freedom.

Unbeknownst to me at the time I joined the American Legion was the fact that the "dominie" of our church was taking a dim view of my action. He considered the Legion a worldly organization. His opinion on this issue was the beginning of an upcoming confrontation between us.

Shortly after I learned about this problem, I realized that the dominie was also criticizing me for my not attending both of the Sunday services. In the evening I generally attended a church service that was being held in the auditorium of the college where I was enrolled prior to my entering military service.

These two issues were of such significance to the pastor that they were taken up at a church consistory meeting. It was decided there that two elders should call on me to iron out my problems. I agreed to meet with these elders; they were friends of my parents. The dominie eventually chose not to accompany the elders.

During this semiformal conference the concerns of the pastor and consistory regarding my association with the American Legion and my lack of attendance at the evening service were relayed to me. I was thoroughly disgusted with the attitudes and principles that were being promulgated by the governing body of a supposedly informed church. Soon after this meeting I wrote the church requesting that my membership be transferred to the Calvin Church, the church that was being held in the college auditorium and the one that I had been attending on Sunday evenings.

It was a couple of months before I received any response from my church regarding my request for the transfer of my membership papers. When I inquired about this lack of response, one of the elders stated that my request was being considered but that there was some concern about a policy that frowned on a member living in the shadow of one church and attending another. I told the elder that I didn't care what the policy was about shadows. I wanted my papers transferred to the church of my choice. Following this confrontation my membership was forwarded to the Calvin Church.

After my papers arrived at the Calvin Church I was, with much courtesy, asked to meet with two it its elders. I was puzzled about why this meeting was being called, but I complied with the request. Both of these elders were professors at the college; the one, Professor Droste, had been my history professor. They were highly respected individuals.

Professor Droste apologetically explained that it was a mandatory procedure for the elders of a church which was the recipient of membership papers of a transferee, to meet with the transferee where there was a problem to solve. He then revealed that attached to my transfer papers was a recommendation for discipline: That I had joined a worldly organization, the American Legion, and that I was not faithful in attending the evening services. After Professor Droste read the charges, both of the elders grinned. They said they could not understand the basis for such charges. Professor Droste said that he too was a member of the American Legion, having served in World War I. As for the Sunday evening services, he stated that attending them was desirable and that they would encourage such attendance but that the absence of regular attendances at the second service as not a matter for disciplinary action. Furthermore, he said, we have seen you here quite often on Sunday evenings. They both essentially apologized for the actions of the Dutton Church and sincerely welcomed me into the fellowship at Calvin.

I had not yet had a successful postwar business venture, but I had another idea. I had heard about a new Kaiser-Frazer automobile that was to be manufactured near Detroit. I went to the designated distributor of this new product; he was in Grand Rapids. After a lengthy discussion he decided to give me a franchise; I promised to build a suitable building. The deal was made, and I then sought franchises for supplemental products. I clinched a deal with the Ferguson Corporation, where I was granted a franchise to sell its farm machinery. I then went to the Hotpoint appliance distributor, and here too I received a franchise. Now all I had to do was to build a building and get to work selling the merchandise.

To build a suitable building I had to obtain a mortgage. My first thought was to make an application for a government (G.I.) Loan through the State

Bank of Caledonia. It was the nearby town where I had attended high school, and it was the bank where I had previously borrowed money. In June of 1940 I had borrowed $125 from the bank to purchase a 1936 V-8 Ford. My brother-in-law, John, had to co-sign for me. I was still a minor. I repaid the loan right on schedule. In November of 1940 I had borrowed $30. I paid this up within the thirty-day limit. In February 1941 I got a loan from the bank for $16.50. This loan was likewise paid on time. I therefore knew that I had a "triple A" credit rating with the Caledonia bank. My best chance for getting a loan seemed to be through this bank; so it was here that I made my application for some money to build.

To get a G.I. loan through a bank, the bank had to get a government-approved appraiser to investigate and approve the intended project, including its location. The appraiser was notified, but he didn't show. I kept calling the bank inquiring about the delay. The bank's manager said he could not understand the lack of response on the part of the appraiser. He, however, said he did not anticipate any problem in getting the loan.

The building had to be built if I was to secure the automobile franchise; so I purchased a lot in Dutton for $900. This left me with a balance in my savings account of about four thousand dollars. I decided to start my building while the busy appraiser was making his rounds.

My first task was to get a mason to lay out the foundation for the building. This was easy. My choice was a very reliable and competent masonry contractor from our church. He took care of the layout immediately, but I encountered a roadblock. I couldn't find a backhoe that was available to dig the area for the required foundation. The only available tool was a hand shovel. I therefore hired a person to help me dig. Together we dug an area three fee deep by three feet wide for a 60' x 80' foundation. When we finished the digging, the masonry contractor faithfully completed this phase of the job.

The blocks, windows, and doors were next. I hired a local block layer, and I assisted him whenever I wasn't running around for materials. When the walls were about one-third up, an authoritative-looking man drove up, got out of his car, and asked for the owner. I told him I was the owner, thinking he was the appraiser. He showed me his credentials. He was from the Office of Price Control. He told me I had to stop using blocks for my building, that all building blocks were restricted for the building of homes.

Needless to say, I became somewhat unsettled. I told him that I had served in the military for almost four years, that I participated in combat, and that I thought one of the freedoms I would enjoy after the war as over was the freedom of trying to create a job for myself so I could survive. He didn't waiver in his demand. He ordered me to stop using the blocks for my building. Soon after the government representative left, I told my block layer to get on with the block laying as fast as he could. Both of us worked late, and on Saturday.

About one week later the representative returned to see if I was complying with his order. The block work on the building was almost complete. He was "ticked," but there seemed to be some hesitancy about serving me with a written citation. He indicated he would go back to the office and make a determination as to what action should be taken. That was the last I heard from him.

After the blocks were up I was out of money. The appraiser still had not shown. I decided to go to the old Kent Bank in downtown Grand Rapids to see if the loan officer there would help me get a loan. First I talked to an underling. He said that there was no chance that the bank would place a mortgage on a building that was so far out from the city limits. He confirmed what his understudy had told me — not a chance. I inquired as to who his superior was. He took me to him. He too, was very kind, but the bottom line was no deal. I finally asked for the person who was the most authoritative officer in the bank. He pointed to a man who appeared to be about eighty years old, sitting at a desk on the balcony floor toward the corner of the building. I requested permission to talk with him. After a short conversation between the bank officer and the elderly gentleman, I was given the nod to come over.

When I approached his desk, he looked at me and then reluctantly suggested that I sit down. I told him I was seeking a loan on a building that was about half completed. I then responded to questions with answers that gave him some of the essentials that every loan officer would want to know. Following this, he slowly interrogated me for about an hour on various matters, including my youth and military service. Finally he said, "Young man, I'm going to take a chance on you. I think I can help you get the eight thousand dollars you need." With this commitment he raised his hand and motioned his expediter to take care of me. With this single motion I was converted from a beggar to a customer.

After signing some papers, I was instructed to go across the street to another building and make arrangements with the appraiser for G.I. loans to make a site check. The bank officer indicated I would have no problem. This worried me. I had heard this before.

I left the bank and went to the office of the appraiser, with a paper in my hand which contained a recommendation of the bank for approval of the loan. The appraiser looked at it himself with words "Dutton, Dutton." He then said, "Oh yes, now I remember." He recalled that the Caledonia bank had recommended disapproval. Because of this, he said, he had made no appraisal. He felt that it would not be totally fair to go to Dutton with a predetermination of disapproval of the site location etc., and to charge a veteran $25 for such useless service. I was later told that the local automobile dealers in Caledonia, where the bank was located, wanted to avoid competition in their service area, which included Dutton.

Once the appraiser had the recommendation of approval in his possession, he viewed the building site and its geographical location within a few days. He promptly approved the loan. This meant the money was mine to use. I completed the building.

There was one more serious problem that had to be solved before the building could be used. I could not find a boiler for the heating unit. None were available. I finally located an old threshing machine steam engine with a boiler on it. With the help of a local junk-yard mechanic we got the thing off the steam engine and into the boiler room. It became the bane of my existence.

Connected to this boiler was a stoker. It forced the coal into the boiler. For some reason, I could never get the apparatus to work properly. It would frequently throw all the sulfur fumes into the boiler room which was built onto the back of the main structure.

During the winter months I would, on my return home from an evening date, stop in at the garage and refill the stoker. The presence of thick sulfur in the boiler room would require me to hold my breath, shovel a couple of shovels full of coal into the stoker and then jump outside to breath. I would repeat this maneuver until the stoker was full.

After the building was completed and I got it operating properly, I made arrangements for opening day. Several ads were placed in the local papers. There was a good turnout, and the day was as successful as could be expected.

Following opening day, reality began to dawn. Salesmen from various companies began to call on me and would display their goods for sale. While I was no neophyte in dealing, having bought and sold some livestock and having operated a small dairy business, I was not prepared for making enlightened decisions regarding the type of merchandise that would sell in a community such as Dutton. I understood the main lines that I would be handling, but any supplemental merchandise that should be stocked was beyond my knowledge and experience. I had very little operating capital, and that capital consisted of borrowed funds. I therefore had to rely somewhat on the salesmen who wanted my business as a continuing account.

While I did not rely completely on the advice of the salesmen, I gave them more credit for honesty than they deserved. Within a short period of time non-saleable items, such as a hand-operated cream separator. At that time, hand separators were no longer generally used. It remained an antique in the show room for a couple of years.

Another reality soon to be experienced was the fact that there were very few people in the area who would frequent a business such as mine. Even the grocery store had limited traffic. Without customers there was little chance of making any sales. Also, public demand for the new Kaiser-Frazer cars was initially nonexistent. To begin with, I was not given any of the 1946 models, although this turned out to be a blessing, as there were several defects in the 1946 models that had to be corrected.

The automotive service section of my business gave me some hope for temporary survival. John, my brother-in-law and your uncle, agreed to head up the repair business. The repair shop wasn't large. It held only six to eight cars. But it was profitable enough to help pay some of the overhead expense.

The Kaiser-Frazer distributor finally delivered to me a couple of automobiles for me to sell. I thought they would move right out to some anxious buyer, but they didn't. No one in my area seemed interested enough to buy this unproven automobile. Everyone seemed to be waiting for the new car that he had ordered through his Ford or Chevrolet dealer. The Ford and Chevrolet automobiles were about a thousand dollars cheaper than the Kaiser at that time, and they were motor vehicles with a proven record.

Having failed in my two previous business attempts, I began to get a gut feeling that this enterprise was also going down the drain. The strain of this distressing thought, combined with my postwar nightmares, was beginning to take its toll on my health. At times, especially at night, I would feel as if my heart was slowing to a stop. I would be awakened during the night with a feeling that there was a total lack of circulation in my body. To overcome this circulatory slowdown, I would force myself to bicycle my legs in the air while lying on my back in bed, in order to get my heart pumping sufficiently fast for me to go back to sleep.

I also experienced some problems during that period of time with dating. I met some lovely girls, but somehow the war had me feeling like an old man. The girls I would meet, while knowing about the war, were seemingly quite unaffected by the reality of it. I naturally didn't want them to be emotionally disturbed by the war. In fact, I had no interest in even talking about it, but the absence of a sense of reality on their part about a catastrophe which had just ended made me feel somewhat estranged from them. The relationship with these girls was somewhat akin to a social relationship between a business man who went bankrupt during the depression and a man who went through the depression with a sizeable trust fund. The latter knew of the depression but he didn't experience it. Because of this emotional chasm between the available young women and myself, I was convinced that it would be difficult for me to find a compatible mate.

Notwithstanding the natural or psychological standoff that existed between myself and the available girls, there were three or four of them that sparked some interest in me. If it hadn't been that my business was apparently going sour at this period in my life, I probably could have given more serious attention to these girls, who were seemingly interested in me. But the problems connected with the business kept my mind occupied day and night.

At one point during this new business venture I realized that I was not going to be able to pay the finance company for the carrying charges on the merchandise that was floor planned and that a failure to pay such charges would make it impossible for me to finance any more cars. I conferred with my brother-in-law John about my shaky financial status. He had four children and could not risk a lack of income. We both agreed on that. He therefore, and rightly so, went back to working for himself in an old nearby vacant garage building.

About a week later I called my Uncle Harry in Kalamazoo, Michigan, and told him of my plight. I apologetically and cautiously inquired whether he would be willing to lend me some money. He said he was coming to Grand Rapids on Saturday and wondered if that would be soon enough to talk about it. It was. Saturday was only two or three days from the call.

During the morning hours on Saturday while my Uncle Harry drove up to the building. I was apprehensive about the meeting. If he would not lend me the money, I didn't know what I would do. After a warm greeting, which my uncle always extended to the members of our family, he asked me how much I needed. I told him I really needed $4,000, but if that was too great a figure I could take less and then try to get some additional funds elsewhere. "Unk" took out his checkbook, wrote me a check for $4,000, and told me to pay him whenever convenient.

After giving me the loan he wanted a ride in the new Kaiser I had on the floor. (I could only place two cars on the show room floor.) I took him for a ride over one of our country roads and told him what I knew about the car. Having been a salesman during his lifetime, he suggested that I learn everything there was to know about the car so that the purchaser would know what he was buying. This made sense. I followed his advice.

Before leaving, he wanted to know how much I would sell him the car for. I pulled out the purchase invoice, and I sold it to him for the exact amount that I had to pay for it. This sale, and the loan, gave my little business some new impetus.

Deciding that I had to do something to draw people to my place of business, I concluded that a public automobile auction would be a good thing to try. Normally automobile auctions were for the car dealers only. An auction where the public could sell and buy would be unique.

I hired a well-known automobile auctioneer, along with his clerk, to conduct the sale. The cars that were to be sold would enter one end of the building (driven by the seller or his driver.) As it approached the auction stand, the auctioneer would sell it. The car would then be driven out of the building to the parking lot, where it would stay until the title was transferred, in my small office, to the purchaser.

While the auction was a drawing card, it wasn't that big of a deal. It had to grow. One day an owner of a radio station came into my office and wanted to sell me some radio time. The net result of his visit was profitable for both of us. I sold him a car and he gave me a few hundred dollars worth of advertising as part payment. The advertisement consisted of live coverage of the auction. This brought traveling car owners right off of the highway to the auction. The auction soon became profitable.

Something else began to work in my favor. Besides my becoming very knowledgeable about the Kaiser-Frazer automobile, there was a growing discontent on the part of the people who had had their orders in for either a new Ford or Chevrolet. These dealers were demanding trade-ins at a low price so they could make a sizeable profit on each deal. This was done in order to avoid violating the rules and regulations of the OPA (Office of Price Administration). Infuriated prospective purchasers began buying Kaiser-Frazer cars. My days of poverty were over — I thought.

Just as I was beginning to sell some cars, the Grand Rapids Kaiser-Frazer distributor, who was also a dealer, cut me off. I evidently was selling cars to his potential customers. Prospective purchasers became aware through the radio publicity of my place of business, which was in a low-overhead area, and not too far from the city. They rightly assumed they could get a better deal in Dutton.

Talking to the distributor, Mr. White, about the matter brought no change. So I called the factory Vice President in charge of sales, person to person, and informed him of my predicament. In response to my complaint he said he would personally be at my place with Mr. White on Monday. He kept his promise. He examined my new building, talked with me for about ten minutes, and then turned to Mr. White an said, "He will have some cars here next week, won't he, Mr. White." Mr. White, of course, confirmed the statement.

My distributor thereafter started to send me cars again. But he soon changed his tactics. He began to make only the Frazer-Manhattans available to me. This was the most expensive car. But I snookered him. I found a dealer near Detroit who would sell me the lower priced cars for only $50 over his cost. So I pulled several of the low-priced cars into Dutton from my new contact and offered them for sale in our local area. This infuriated Mr. White, but he knew that he had it coming. He resumed selling me the lower-priced cars and the regular Frazers.

My money troubles were for the most part behind me. At this point Mr. White offered me a job, wanting me to close my Dutton dealership and to take a job with him where I would be in charge of sales for all of Western Michigan. I declined his offer.

A partner was what I now needed, one with mechanical ability. My brother-in-law John had developed a small but successful body shop in the nearby garage he had rented, where he did all of the bodywork for my business as well as for other dealers. So I invited another person whom I had previously asked, to join me. He accepted.

My interests were now broadened by the suggestions of a friend who had previously worked with me and who now wanted to go into home building. He chose the plans and build one house as a starter. We made a little money on that one. Then Mr. White, the distributor, wanted us to build him a commercial building to store automobiles and parts. This we did, for 10% of the costs. He tried to hide some for the costs, but we detected the variance and made him cough up the rest of the money.

My friend then convinced me that we should build three more houses. I agreed. With this commitment having been made, I took off on a much-needed vacation trip. When I returned, my friend had six foundations laid, three with basements. This meant I had to borrow money again. All of this would not have been so bad, but during the building of these houses my friend forgot to brace the basement walls. A storm erupted during the construction of these houses. The rain caused a mud slide against the walls , which in turn caused two of the houses to fall into their own basements.

With this housing project in a state of disaster, my friend decided, and rightly so, that there would be no profit in this venture. Broke from having been in a previous unsuccessful business, he decided to take off for Florida, where he hoped to get a job where he could earn some money and send for his family. Thereafter I personally supervised a complete reconstruction of these houses as well as having to personally dig the sanitary sewers with a shovel, in clay land. I finally got the houses completed, but then they wouldn't sell. Ultimately I sold them on land contracts which I had to hold for several years.

My social life was continually progressing. There was one occasion that should be of special interest to you. A tall friend of mine invited me to go with him as a guest to what was known as the "Wee High Club." It was for men over six feet tall and women over five feet eight inches. During that evening I saw an attractive girl who had a very pleasant smile. She was in constant conversation with some friends of hers. I didn't get to meet her at that meeting, but I learned that she lived in Grand Rapids and that she had recently moved with her parents to a new home near Dutton. I was informed also that she was not a member of the club. The chances were that I would never meet her again unless I would get up enough courage to give her a telephone call.

One day I got brave enough to make that call. I introduced myself. She knew who I was. She had seen me play ball, and she was aware of my place of business. After a few verbal pleasantries over the phone I asked her if she would like to go out to dinner. She said she would like that very much.

When I went to pick her up for our first date, I thought I should use the front door of their country home. I learned later that no one ever used the front door. Everyone used the side door, which led directly into the opposite end of the living room. As soon as I was let in the front door, it was obvious that the other door was the one I should have used. This made me feel rather awkward. But there I was, in the house. I introduced myself to this new and exciting person. Her name was Lois.

Due to the fact that my postwar dating up to this time had produced no promising results, I had no high expectations for any permanent relationship with this new acquaintance. But one date led to another. We always seemed to have a good time together, even though our cultural backgrounds were somewhat dissimilar. We were also opposites in so many ways, but the chemistry was there.

Not only was this new attractive friend an intelligent and witty girl, she was also a person who had experienced the reality of war. Her former fiance, who was an army pilot, was killed in 1944 in the European theatre of war. This sobering event undoubtedly deepened her concept of life and caused her to have a maturity that I found lacking in some of the other female friends with whom I had become acquainted.

During our courtship I was always pleased with the attention that I would receive from this new girl friend, but I was reluctant to believe that I could be number one in her life. One day while I was in my office at my place of business in Dutton, an automobile that I recognized drove up to the front door. It was Lois'. She was alone. She obviously had come to see me. Knowing her inherent hesitancy about doing something like this I was convinced that she was sincerely interested in me. Serious thoughts began to take root within me. Finally, one night during a dinner date, I mustered up enough courage to ask this beautiful girl if she would marry me. I had the ring in my pocket in case she would say yes. She accepted my proposal, whereupon I took the ring from my pocket and placed it on her finger. She was ecstatic.

After taking her home and saying good night, I drove down the long driveway toward the road. As I was about to enter the highway, I glanced back at the house. I saw a light go on in her parents' bedroom. I knew she had awakened them to tell them the news.

Never having been satisfied with being in the automobile and farm-equipment business and always having wanted to get a college degree, I decided to sell my business and return to school. I sold my business on a time-payment contract to my partner for the cost of the equipment and automotive parts and traded my building for a large old castle-like home at 233 College Avenue SE, a ritzy section of Grand Rapids. The new owner of my building then leased it back to my former partner so he could continue in business.

Having lived with my parents for over two and a half years following the war, and now having a home of my own, I decided to move. Immediately I began to convert the old home into apartments. I anticipated that my fiancee and I would live in one of the apartments after our marriage.

Chapter XIX.

Return To College

At the age of twenty-eight I decided to resume my education. It took two years to get my BA degree (1951) and an additional three years for my Juris Doctorate (1954). During the time I was pursuing my undergraduate degree my finance, Lois, decided to audit a class during the summer months at Calvin College, where I was attending. I accused her of taking this course just so she could keep an eye on me, which I wanted to believe.

The College Avenue home.

Chapter XX.

A Meaningful Marriage

It was amidst all of this transition and activity that my fiancee, Lois, and I set the date of June 30, 1950, as our wedding date.

The wedding took place in the Olivet United Brethern Church. A minister of the Calvin Christian Reformed Church, one of the more progressive CRC churches, and the church where I was then a member, performed the ceremony. The ritual itself was traditional and meaningful.

It was a sizeable wedding. The church was quite full. Protocol was not strictly adhered to. Ma was very ill with either arteriosclerosis, or what we now believe was Alzheimer's disease. She was seated in the back row with Pa. Grandma Bastianse (Reminga before her first husband died), Ma's mother, stood in the reception line for Ma.

A newspaper report of our wedding was as follows:

Lois Solomon Weds Russell H. Volkema

Lois Jean Solomon, daughter of Mr. and Mrs. Lewis A. Solomon, Sixtieth St., became the bride of Russell H. Volkema, son of Mr. and Mrs. Andrew Volkema of Dutton, Friday evening at Olivet church. Rev. Clarence Boomsma officiated.

Peonies, gladioli, palms, and candelabra decorated the altar; Mrs. Lyle B. Willis played the traditional wedding music and accompanied Simon Oppenhuizen, who sang "Through the Years," "Because," and the "Lord's Prayer."

The bride chose a white gown of imported Chantilly lace and satin fashioned with a high neckline of illusion in a scalloped motif, which was repeated in the large circular train. The bodice was tightly fitted and the long lace sleeves tapered to points over the wrists. Her finger-tip-length veil was secured by a coronet embroidered with seed pearls. She carried a bouquet of white stephanotis and swainsona.

The matron of honor, Mrs. Ernest J. Schmidt, sister of the bride, wore a delphinium-blue organdy dress over white taffeta with matching hat and mitts. She carried a bouquet of pink roses, delphinium, and swainsona.

Attired in Organdy

The bridesmaids, Mrs. Henry Horstmanshof, sister of the bride, and Mrs. Richard LaBrenz, were attired in delphinium-blue organdy gowns over pale blue taffeta slips designed like that of the matron of honor. They also wore matching hats and mitts and carried bouquets of roses, delphinium, and swainsonia. Ruth Volkema and Shirley VanLaar, nieces of the bridegroom, were flower girls. They wore white organdy gowns over white taffeta slips, and matching bonnets.

Francis Volkema was the best man. The ushers were Robert Solomon of Detroit, brother of the bride, and Jay Wiltzer. Mr. and Mrs. Alger Paauw of Chicago were master and mistress of ceremonies. Mrs. Paauw chose a beige crepe gown and white glamelia corsage.

The bride's mother wore a navy-blue crepe-and-lace dress with navy accessories and a corsage of pink roses and stephanotis.

A reception was held in the church parlors. Lois Williams of Kalamazoo sang "If God Left Only You" and Grieg's "I Love Thee." Mrs. Gerrit Van Ringelsteyn and Mrs. Alfred Brown played violin and piano selections. Elaine Reynolds assisted about the rooms.

After a northern wedding trip the couple will be at home at 233 College Avenue. For going away the bride wore a pale-blue marquise dress with navy accessories and a white glamelia corsage.

Out-of-town guests were Mrs. Robert Solomon of Detroit, Mrs. John Barnett of Hastings, Charles Gordon of Chicago, and Mr. and Mrs. Erwin Peters of Indianapolis.

After the reception your mother and I went to Traverse City, Michigan, for a few days. On returning from Traverse City, we began our life together by living in one of the apartments in the old castle-like home. I continued in college. Your mother resumed her teaching duties at Buchanan Grade School. Our honeymoon to Quebec, Canada, was delayed for about a month due to my schedule at college.

It was from this marriage that you four children were brought into this world. We have always been, and still are, thankful for having been so blessed.

It is my hope and the hope of your mother that you and your families will be beneficiaries of God's blessings throughout your entire lives.

Love Dad

My fiance-your mother.